# LAW OF THE LAND

## A Practical Legal Guide for Tourists and Business Travelers

# Egypt

*By Michael L. Moore Esq.*

Edited by Ally Knez-Siddique

Cover Design: Kristina Conatser

Published by: Law of the Land Publishing LLC

ISBN: 978-1-964870-20-5

# DEDICATION

This book is dedicated to the memory of my late older brother, Kenneth Lee Moore, whose tragic murder at 15 years of age inspired me to write this series of books.

This book is also dedicated to my parents, John Henry Moore, and Edna Mae Moore, whose tremendous parenting skills kept me focused on the important things in life: being reverent, getting educated, and prioritizing family.

Finally, this book is dedicated to my beautiful family, my wife Royellen, my son AJ, and my daughter Karla. They inspire me every single day to be kind, patient, and compassionate.

## IN LOVING MEMORY OF:

Belinda Joyce Moore Moss—my beautiful and wonderful sister, who supported me in every positive thing that I ever attempted to do.

Michael Eugene Baker—my dedicated and loyal friend and brother, who always wanted the very best for me.

Sylvia Joyce Hill—my eldest sister, who had a beautiful spirit and was like a second mother to me.

# LAW OF THE LAND ®

**PUBLISHING for Tourists & Business Travelers**

## Travel smart. Stay legal. Stay safe.®

### From local laws to medical guides we've got you covered world wide
### in one digital platform.

# PREFACE

My introduction to the justice system came when I was only 10 years old. My 15-year-old brother was murdered with a butcher knife by a 19-year-old in a simple argument over a torn shirt. I was devastated by his death and sought retribution for his fate that never came. The woman was initially charged with second degree murder, but after plea negotiations, she was convicted of manslaughter and sentenced to only five years in a youthful offender school and ordered to undergo psychiatric care. That was it. Nothing more. The judicial system had run its course.

My family knew nothing about the justice system, and we did not have the tools to advocate for ourselves. No one provided us with a written source to reference for guidance through this process. There was no easily accessible, easy to understand, definitive source to educate ourselves about the legal system that we suddenly and unexpectedly found ourselves immersed in after being victimized by such a violent criminal act.

As I got older, finished college, law school, and ultimately started practicing law, it became clear to me that most people are not knowledgeable about the law or how the judicial process works. If most people are uninformed here in the United States regarding the law and the legal process, how would they fare when in other countries? I realized that tourists and businesspeople who travel internationally needed access to information on how to navigate the legal system in other countries!

For many years, there has been considerable media attention focused on international travelers experiencing legal difficulties while traveling abroad. Most of these news stories gained attention in the United States and abroad because they involved American citizens facing punishment that was considered "unconventional" and "harsh" by United States' legal standards. I recall a news story in 1994 regarding Michael Fay, a young American male, who had broken the law in Singapore. He was convicted and sentenced to be caned and or whipped publicly. While the United States Government weighed in on the inappropriate and cruel nature of the punishment, the young American was beaten because he had been convicted under Singapore law.

Similarly, in recent years, international news stories have garnered headlines regarding foreign travelers and their issues with the laws of countries that were not their own. Amanda Knox, an American woman, was accused of murdering her roommate in Italy in 2007 and spent almost four years in an Italian prison before being definitively acquitted by the Supreme Court of Cassatio. Kenneth Bae, an American citizen, was arrested in North Korea in 2012 and was convicted for hostile acts against the communist country. He was sentenced to 15 years hard labor but was released in 2014 after efforts by the U.S. State Department. More recently, United States Basketball Star, Brittany Griner was arrested in February 2022 at a Moscow airport on drug-related charges and detained for nearly 10 months, spending much of that time in prison. Her plight unfolded at the same time Russia invaded Ukraine and further heightened tensions between Russia and the United States, ending only after she was freed in exchange for a notorious Russian arms dealer.

It was in 1994 that another personal tragic event occurred that finally inspired me to write these series of books. A dear friend and also client of mine was brutally murdered while on his second honeymoon in Jamaica. News of his murder shocked me and our local community. The legal hurdles his family had to overcome to see that justice was properly dispensed far away from home, in another country, with an entirely different set of criminal procedural rules and laws, was difficult to navigate.

As I was my friend's attorney at the time of his death, his family asked that I act as their "legal liaison" to the Jamaican Prosecutor's Office and to the Jamaican Police Department. I participated in multiple police interviews with my client's widow because she was the primary witness to his murder. As a former prosecuting attorney, I was also allowed by the Court, as a professional courtesy, to sit at the prosecutor's table to consult with the prosecuting attorney during trial. What I observed about the Jamaican trial process from a front row seat was compelling enough to cause me to seriously consider educating the "world" regarding what to expect and how to act appropriately when faced with legal issues while traveling abroad.

One of the realities in life is that, regardless of what country you are in, it is never a pleasant experience to run afoul of the law and be forced to accept that someone else will be making a decision about your pecuniary, proprietary, or penal interests (your money, your property, or your freedom).

It is important to know what the laws are, how they apply to you, and how to navigate the legal system if you are charged with a crime. It is also very helpful to know what resources are available to you if you are the victim of a criminal act. At the end of the day, an "ounce of prevention is worth a pound of cure," so the more knowledge you have, the more ammunition you possess, and the more likely you will have a positive outcome.

If you are traveling to Egypt, the first thing you should pack is a copy of this book! The helpful information and tips contained in this volume will provide a great starting point for knowing what to do (and not to do!) when you arrive at your destination and will help ensure that you have a wonderful vacation or business trip unmarred by tangles with the law.

# TABLE OF CONTENTS

# INTRODUCTION

# INTRODUCTION

As a practicing attorney for over 34 years, I have encountered numerous clients who travel often, but are unaware of the laws of the land they are traveling to.

Therefore, many years ago, I decided to write a series of books that would explain the laws of specific countries. My focus was to explain the laws that may affect travelers in a straightforward manner, without all of the legal language that is sometimes hard for even seasoned attorneys to understand.

## About This Book

The aim of this book is simple. It provides you, the traveler, with a simple, easy to read book that will provide a basic legal guide that explains the law in the country that you are about to visit. It is not intended to educate you on ALL of the laws in a given country. The goal is to provide you with the details of the most common legal and safety issues faced by tourists and business travelers.

I have also provided context with background information on places not to visit, statistics on the country and prevention measures you should take to safeguard your legal and physical safety. Knowledge is a powerful thing and knowing how to stay out of trouble (or how to get out of it!) is important for everyone who travels.

This *Law of The Land/Egypt* book simply helps you become more informed about your legal rights, responsibilities, and obligations in a wide range of subject areas.

Last, but not least, this book does NOT purport to offer legal advice. It does, however, provide the information you need to stay safe, follow the law and navigate around legal difficulties. However, if you do face legal difficulties, the information in this book will provide you with a starting point for solving the problem and obtaining legal assistance should it be required.

## Hypotheticals Used Throughout This Book

From time to time throughout this book, I will explain the law to readers by using hypothetical scenarios. These hypotheticals will be marked by an icon that will be explained in further detail as you read on.

## How This Book is Organized

CHAPTER 1: **About Egypt.** This chapter will provide you with a brief overview about Egypt and its history. It also addresses Visa requirements, monetary advice, and the best times to visit.

CHAPTER 2: **Customs.** This chapter will provide information on what to expect when entering Egypt. It will also explain what restricted and prohibited items are when entering Egypt along with custom's regulations.

CHAPTER 3: **Crime in Egypt.** This chapter provides an overview of the history of crime in Egypt and steps that Egypt's officials have taken to curb the high rate of crime.

CHAPTER 4: **Criminal Law Violations.** This chapter will provide information on drug offenses, penalties, true events and questions and answers.

CHAPTER 5: **Alcohol-Related Offenses.** This chapter will provide key points regarding the sale, consumption, and regulations of alcohol use in Egypt.

CHAPTER 6: **Firearm & Ammunition Offenses.** This chapter will provide key points regarding the possession of firearms and ammunition in Egypt.

CHAPTER 7: **Prostitution.** This chapter provides an overview of the history of prostitution in Egypt, laws and penalties, prostitution practices, sex trafficking, sex tourism, health in Egypt, tips to avoid being hassled, a Law of the Land Hypothetical, and the current situation on prostitution in Egypt.

CHAPTER 8: **LGBTQ.** This chapter will provide information regarding the acceptance of LGBTQ people in Egypt and the laws surrounding homosexuality.

CHAPTER 9: **Sexually Motivated/Violent Crimes.** This chapter will provide an overview of sexually related crimes in Egypt.

CHAPTER 10: **Arrested in Egypt.** This chapter will provide information on what to do if you are arrested in Egypt.

CHAPTER 11: **Jails vs. Prisons: Conditions & Culture.** This chapter will provide information on the conditions and culture of Egyptian Jails and Prisons.

CHAPTER 12: **Helping a Friend or Relative Imprisoned in Egypt.** This chapter will provide information on how you can assist a friend or relative imprisoned in Egypt.

CHAPTER 13: **The Administration of Justice.** This chapter will provide information on Egypt's Legal System.

CHAPTER 14: **Crime Victim Assistance.** This chapter will provide information on crime victim assistance along with providing safety tips.

CHAPTER 15: **Police.** This chapter will provide information on Police in Egypt and how to report a crime.

CHAPTER 16: **How to Get Legal Help in Egypt.** This chapter will provide information regarding how to obtain legal assistance for travelers to Egypt.

CHAPTER 17: **Medical Facilities & Hospitals.** This chapter will provide information about how to obtain medical care while visiting Egypt.

CHAPTER 18: **Driving in Egypt.** This chapter will provide information on driving in Egypt, it's traffic rules, and road safety tips.

CHAPTER 19: **Nude Beaches & Clothing-Optional Resorts.** This chapter will provide an overview of nude beaches and clothing-optional resorts in Egypt, and the legality and safety of visiting nude beaches in Egypt.

CHAPTER 20: **Unusual Laws.** This chapter will provide information on some Unusual Laws in Egypt, and penalties and fines.

CHAPTER 21: **Traveling Safely.** This chapter will provide information on women traveling alone, crime prevention for families, safety notes for all travelers, and overall advice.

CHAPTER 22: **Tourist Taxation.** This chapter will provide information on taxes that tourists are required to pay in Egypt.

CHAPTER 23: **Long-Term Stays.** This chapter will provide an overview of the consequences for overstaying your visit to Egypt.

CHAPTER 24: **Civil Litigation.** This chapter will provide information about the civil litigation process in Egypt.

CHAPTER 25: **Other Things to Know.** This chapter will provide information on the harassment of tourists, travel and safety, and other practical tips.

CHAPTER 26: **Quick Reference Guide.** This chapter is a quick way to get information. It is a condensed version of the chapters in this book.

**Emergency/Important Contact Numbers in Egypt**

**Useful Arabic Phrases**

**Glossary**

## Icons Used in this Book

What do those pictures throughout the book mean? See below:

 WARNING: This icon flags information about things you should **avoid** while visiting Egypt. Heed the advice next to this icon to avoid legal perils.

 REMEMBER: This icon flags noteworthy information that you **shouldn't forget.**

 HELPFUL TIPS: This icon flags information that will help you when entering Egypt, relates to a legal situation, or refers to resources available while visiting Egypt.

 TECHNICAL INFORMATION: This icon flags technical aspects of the law. If you are faced with a legal problem, and you want to learn more about the law involved, this information can be helpful.

 **ADDITIONAL INFORMATION**: This icon points to the location of additional information available on the internet.

 **HYPOTHETICAL**: This icon points to hypothetical scenarios to illustrate possible legal problems and the outcome.

 **QUESTIONS**: This icon points to questions and answers throughout the book.

 **TRUE STORY**: This icon points to true events throughout the book.

## Where to Go From Here

If you have a specific question about the law in Egypt as it relates to a particular area, just turn to the chapter that addresses that issue, or turn to the Quick Reference Guide. You can also read the book from cover to cover to obtain a more comprehensive understanding of Egyptian laws and resources available should you find yourself in a legal predicament while visiting.

 **Disclaimer:** While the recommendations in this book primarily address U.S. citizens, the information is relevant and applicable to citizens of any country.

# ABOUT EGYPT

- About Egypt
- Egypt, the Basics
- Egyptian Hospitality

# ABOUT EGYPT

## About Egypt

Egypt is located in **northeastern Africa**, with the Sinai Peninsula extending into Asia, making it a transcontinental country. It is bordered by the Mediterranean Sea to the north, the Red Sea to the east, Libya to the west, Sudan to the south, and Israel and the Gaza Strip to the northeast. Egypt covers about **1 million square kilometers (386,000 square miles)**, making it the **30th largest country in the world**. As of 2024, Egypt has a population of over **111 million people**, making it the most populous country in the Arab world.

Egypt is world-renowned for its ancient civilization. Tourists from across the globe come to visit iconic landmarks like the pyramids of **Giza, the Great Sphinx, the Valley of the Kings,** and **the Nile River**. It is considered one of the birthplaces of human civilization and has greatly influenced art, architecture, language, and religion throughout history. Today, Egypt is known not only for its archaeological wonders, but also for its **rich blend of Arab, African, and Mediterranean cultures, colorful markets**, and **unique cuisine.**

Egypt's history stretches back over 5,000 years. It was unified under the first pharaoh around 3100 BCE and flourished for millennia as a major ancient kingdom. It was later conquered by **Persians, Greeks** (under Alexander the Great), **Romans,** and **eventually Arab Muslims** in the 7th century CE. It was **part of the Ottoman Empire,** followed by a period of **British control** until Egypt gained independence in the 20th century. The 1952 revolution ended the monarchy and established a republic. Modern Egypt has experienced major political shifts, including the 2011 Arab Spring, but remains a major cultural and political force in the Middle East and North Africa.

## *The Capital*

**Cairo,** the capital of Egypt, lies along the Nile River and is the **largest city in both Africa and the Middle East**, with **over 20 million residents** in the metro area. Cairo serves as Egypt's political, economic, and cultural hub. It is home to the national government, major universities, religious institutions, and international organizations.

Cairo is famous for its proximity to the Giza pyramids and the ancient city of Memphis. The city blends Islamic architecture, 19th-century European-style boulevards, and modern skyscrapers. Key attractions include the Egyptian Museum, Khan el-Khalili bazaar, and Al-Azhar Mosque. The city is busy and chaotic, but its energy and history make it unforgettable.

## *The People*

Egyptians are known for being welcoming, family-oriented, and deeply connected to their history. The population is primarily **ethnic Egyptian**, with minority groups including **Nubians** in the south, **Bedouin** communities in desert areas, and smaller numbers of **Greeks**, **Armenians, and others**. Most Egyptians live along the Nile River or in urban centers like Cairo and Alexandria, though many rural communities still follow traditional agricultural lifestyles.

**Hospitality** is a core value in Egyptian culture, and social life often revolves around food, music, and extended family. Egyptians are proud of their national identity, ancient heritage, and cultural traditions that have been passed down for generations.

## Language

The official language of Egypt is Arabic, specifically **Egyptian Arabic**, which is the most widely spoken dialect and also understood across much of the Arab world. Modern Standard Arabic is used in formal writing, news, and education. However, **English** is taught in schools and is widely used in business and tourism. While many Egyptians in tourist areas speak basic English, proficiency may vary in rural or less-developed regions.

## Religion

**Islam is the state religion of Egypt**, and around **90%** of the population are **Sunni Muslims.** Islamic traditions are deeply woven into everyday life, from daily prayer times to major religious festivals such as Ramadan and Eid al-Fitr. Religious values often shape family roles, dress, and social etiquette.

Approximately **10%** of the population are **Christians**, mostly belonging to the Coptic Orthodox Church, which has existed in Egypt since the early centuries of Christianity. Religious holidays and customs are publicly observed and respected across much of the country, and mosques and churches are prominent parts of Egypt's landscape.

## Affordability

Egypt is considered **very affordable** by international standards, especially for travelers from North America and Europe. For example, a midrange hotel room typically costs **$40–$70 USD per night**, while budget travelers can find hostels or simple guesthouses for as low as **$10–$20 USD per night.** Luxury hotels and Nile cruises range from **$100–$300 USD per night**, depending on the level of service and location. Likewise, local street food like falafel, koshari, or shawarma often costs only **$1–$3 USD.** Meals in casual sit-down restaurants range from **$4–$8 USD**, and upscale dining may run between **$15–$25 USD per person**. Egypt's public transportation is also inexpensive: a metro ride in Cairo costs about **$0.15–$0.30 USD**, and taxis or Uber rides usually cost **$1–$5 USD** within cities. Intercity travel by bus or train ranges from **$3–$15 USD**, while short domestic flights can be found for **$40–$90 USD**, depending on the route and time of booking.

Overall, Egypt offers exceptional value for money and remains one of the most budget-friendly destinations for history lovers, adventure seekers, and cultural travelers.

## Egypt, the Basics

*How to Get There?*

Egypt is well connected to the rest of the world by air, and flying is the most common and convenient way to reach the country. Direct international flights land in several major Egyptian cities, with **Cairo International Airport** (**CAI**) serving as the main international gateway. It is the busiest airport in Egypt and one of the largest in Africa, located about 14 miles (22 km) northeast of central Cairo. Other major international airports include:

- **Hurghada International Airport** (**HRG**): Located on the Red Sea coast, popular with European tourists for beach resorts and diving.
- **Sharm El-Sheikh International Airport** (**SSH**): Another Red Sea airport, known for luxury resorts, snorkeling, and all-inclusive packages.
- **Borg El Arab Airport** (**HBE**): Serves Alexandria and the northern Mediterranean coast.
- **Luxor International Airport** (**LXR**): Serves Upper Egypt and is used by travelers visiting ancient temples and tombs.

Many international airlines fly to Egypt, including **EgyptAir** (the national carrier), **Turkish Airlines, Qatar Airways, Lufthansa, Air France, Emirates, Etihad, British Airways**, and several budget airlines like **easyJet** and **Wizz Air** for intra-European travel. Direct flights from the U.S. are limited but often connect through European or Gulf hubs (such as Frankfurt, Istanbul, or Doha).

*Cheapest Times to Fly*

The most affordable time to fly to Egypt is typically during the **summer months of June through August**, when airfare from North America and Europe can drop significantly—though this coincides with extreme heat in much of the country. Round-trip tickets from the U.S. can range from **$600–$900 USD** in summer, while peak season fares (December–January and March–April) often cost **$1,000–$1,400 USD** or more. **Booking 2–3 months in advance** generally yields the best prices. Flights to resort destinations like Hurghada and Sharm El-Sheikh may be cheaper through European carriers offering seasonal discounts.

*When to Visit?*

The best time to visit Egypt is from **October to April**, when the weather is cooler and more pleasant, especially for exploring historic sites like the pyramids, temples, and tombs. During these months, daytime temperatures typically range from **60°F to 80°F (15°C to 27°C)**, which is ideal for sightseeing without the discomfort of extreme heat.

The **peak tourist season** is **December through February**, when crowds are at their highest and prices for flights and accommodations rise. For a more relaxed experience with fewer tourists and still-comfortable weather, the **shoulder months of October, November, and April** are excellent choices. These months offer the best balance of good weather, smaller crowds, and reasonable prices.

 # Do I Need a Visa?

**Most travelers do need a visa to enter Egypt**, including U.S. citizens. American travelers can either apply for an e-visa online before their trip through Egypt's official **e-visa portal** (https://www.visa2egypt.gov.eg) or get a **visa on arrival** at major airports such as Cairo, Hurghada, or Sharm El-Sheikh.

The tourist visa typically allows a stay of **up to 30 days** and costs **$25 USD for a single-entry visa** or **$60 USD for a multiple-entry visa.** E-visas should be requested at least seven days before arrival, and your passport must be valid for at least six months beyond your intended date of entry. Travelers from certain countries may need to apply in advance at an Egyptian embassy or consulate, so it's important to check the latest entry requirements for your nationality before traveling.

*How to Get Around*

Getting around Egypt as a tourist is relatively easy, with several convenient and affordable transportation options depending on where you're traveling. In major cities like Cairo and Alexandria, **the metro** is one of the fastest and cheapest ways to move around, with fares typically under $0.30 USD. **Taxis** and **ride-hailing apps** like Uber and Careem are widely available in urban areas and offer an inexpensive and reliable way to get around, with most rides costing between $1 and $5 USD. In tourist-heavy cities like Luxor and Aswan, **horse-drawn carriages** and **tuk-tuks** are also common for short distances and sightseeing.

For longer trips between cities, Egypt has an **extensive network of buses and trains.** The trains are especially popular for traveling between Cairo, Alexandria, and Upper Egypt, with sleeper trains available for overnight routes to Luxor and Aswan. Prices vary based on class and destination, but overnight train tickets typically range from $30 to $80 USD. Domestic **flights** are also a convenient option for covering long distances quickly—especially between Cairo and Red Sea resorts like Sharm El-Sheikh or Hurghada—with prices usually ranging from $40 to $90 USD if booked in advance.

In coastal or resort areas, many travelers walk, rent bikes, or rely on hotel-arranged shuttles. While driving is possible, most visitors prefer not to rent cars due to local traffic conditions and unpredictable road rules, especially in busy cities.

## Monetary Advice

The national currency of Egypt is the **Egyptian Pound** (**EGP**). As of mid-2025, the exchange rate is approximately **48 EGP to 1 USD**, though this may fluctuate, so it's wise to check current rates before traveling. U.S. dollars and euros are sometimes accepted in tourist-heavy areas like hotels, upscale restaurants, or souvenir shops, but you should expect to use Egyptian pounds for most purchases, especially in local markets and smaller establishments.

Credit cards are widely accepted in hotels, large stores, and modern restaurants, especially in Cairo, Alexandria, and Red Sea resorts. However, many smaller businesses, taxis, and local eateries operate on a **cash-only basis**, so it's important to carry some Egyptian pounds with you. ATMs are common in cities and tourist areas, and most international cards work, though some may charge a small fee for withdrawals.

Bargaining is a **common and expected** part of shopping in Egypt, particularly in bazaars, markets, and when buying souvenirs. It's not considered rude—rather, it's part of the cultural experience. Start by offering about half of the initial asking price and negotiate from there with a friendly attitude.

Tipping, or "**baksheesh,**" is a normal part of Egyptian culture and often expected. In restaurants, a tip of **10–15%** is customary if service isn't already included. Hotel staff, drivers, tour guides, and even bathroom attendants may expect a small tip—typically **5 to 20 EGP** (about **$0.10–$0.40 USD**) depending on the service. While it's not mandatory, tipping is appreciated and often supplements low base wages. Carrying small bills makes it easier to tip appropriately.

## Egyptian Hospitality

Egypt is widely known for its remarkable hospitality, which is deeply ingrained in its culture and social life. Egyptians take great pride in being

**warm and generous hosts**, often going to great lengths to make visitors feel welcome and valued. Hospitality is not just a casual gesture but a vital part of everyday interactions, reflecting respect, kindness, and community spirit.

When expressing their hospitality, Egyptians typically greet guests warmly, offering tea, coffee, sweets, or even full meals as a way to honor and include them. It's common for hosts to insist that visitors stay longer and accept multiple servings, seeing this as a sign of goodwill and friendship. Invitations to share food or spend time together are often extended even to new acquaintances, highlighting the openness and generosity characteristic of Egyptian culture. Accepting food or drink when offered is seen as respectful and appreciative, while refusing can unintentionally offend the host.

Egyptians appreciate patience and a genuine interest in their customs, and dressing modestly, especially in religious or traditional settings, is considered a mark of respect. It's impolite to show impatience, engage in public displays of affection, or discuss sensitive topics unless invited. Respect for prayer times and asking permission before taking photographs also demonstrate cultural sensitivity.

Understanding that hospitality is a core value helps you appreciate the time and effort Egyptians dedicate to making guests feel at home. This openness and warmth create a welcoming environment that leaves a lasting positive impression on travelers.

# CUSTOMS

# CUSTOMS

## Travelers Entering Egypt

To enter Egypt, your passport must be valid for at least six months beyond your planned entry date and have at least one blank page for stamps. Most travelers, including U.S. citizens, need a visa to enter Egypt. As mentioned above, you can obtain a 30-day tourist visa upon arrival at major airports by paying a fee of about $25 USD, usually accepted in U.S. dollars, euros, or British pounds. If you are visiting the Sinai Peninsula (places like Sharm El Sheikh, Dahab, Nuweiba, or Taba) for less than 15 days, you can get a free entry permission stamp upon arrival. However, for stays longer than 15 days or travel outside the Sinai, a visa is required. Some travelers might need a yellow fever vaccination certificate depending on their previous travel history, so it's wise to check with the Egyptian embassy or consulate before traveling.

When you land in Egypt, after disembarking from the plane, follow signs to immigration. If you have not obtained a visa beforehand, you will need to pay for a visa on arrival at a dedicated counter. Present your passport, visa (if you have it in advance), and a completed arrival card to the immigration officer. Then collect your luggage at the baggage claim area and proceed through customs, where random checks may occur. It's important to stay vigilant, especially in crowded places, and be mindful of your belongings.

 For the latest travel advisories and safety information, you can visit the **U.S. Department of State's Egypt Travel Advisory** page at **https://travel.state.gov/content/travel/ en/international-travel/International-Travel-Country-Information-Pages/Egypt.html**

## Customs Entitlements and Monetary Restrictions

When entering Egypt, travelers should be aware of certain customs and monetary restrictions to ensure a smooth process. You are allowed to bring up to $10,000 US dollars or its equivalent in other foreign currencies without declaring it, but any amount above this must be declared upon arrival. For the local currency, Egyptian Pounds, the limit is 5,000 EGP. It is recommended to exchange money only through official banks or licensed exchange offices to comply with Egyptian laws.

Personal items such as clothing, electronics, and gifts are permitted without customs duties as long as they are for personal use and not in commercial quantities. Bringing large quantities of the same item could raise suspicion of commercial intent. Some items, like used passenger vehicles, may have special restrictions and require permits.

Likewise, when leaving Egypt, travelers may carry up to 10,000 US dollars or equivalent foreign currency and up to 5,000 Egyptian Pounds. Personal items like clothing and electronics are generally allowed, but exporting goods such as gold and silver purchased in Egypt may be restricted unless they are for personal use and in small quantities.

## Restricted and Prohibited Items[1]

When traveling to Egypt, certain items are restricted or prohibited to protect security, public health, and cultural norms. Here's an overview of what you generally cannot or should not bring into Egypt:

*Prohibited Items:*

- **Narcotics and illegal drugs:** Strictly banned with severe penalties.
- **Weapons and ammunition:** Including firearms, knives, explosives, and replicas.
- **Pornographic materials:** Any explicit or obscene content.
- **Religious materials that might offend:** Anything considered blasphemous or offensive to Islam or Egyptian culture.
- **Counterfeit goods:** Fake branded products.
- **Certain plants and animals:** Without proper permits to prevent ecological harm.

*Restricted Items:*

- **Large amounts of cash or monetary instruments:** Must be declared if over the limit.
- **Medicines:** Some prescription drugs require a doctor's prescription or import permit.
- **Electronic equipment:** Sometimes customs will check for professional or commercial quantities.
- **Food products:** Limited to avoid risks from pests or contamination.
- **Cultural artifacts and antiques:** Export and import are strictly controlled.

---

1    https://www.egyptsevisa.org/
     egypt-customs-regulations-guide-to-entry-exit-and-travel-essentials

Bringing prohibited or restricted items into Egypt can lead to serious consequences. These may include confiscation of the items by customs authorities, fines, or even arrest and criminal charges depending on the severity of the violation. In some cases, travelers can face detention or deportation. It is important to declare any restricted items and ensure you have the necessary permits to avoid legal trouble.

If you are unsure about any items, it is best to check with the Egyptian embassy or customs officials before traveling.

 ## Five Practical Tips to Know Before You Go

- **Respect Local Dress Codes:** In Egypt, especially when visiting religious sites like mosques or traditional neighborhoods, dressing modestly is important. For women, covering shoulders and knees and carrying a scarf to cover the head if needed shows respect. Men should avoid wearing sleeveless shirts in such places.

- **Learn Basic Arabic Greetings:** Simple phrases like "Salam Alaikum" (Peace be upon you) and "Shukran" (Thank you) go a long way in showing respect and friendliness to locals. Egyptians appreciate visitors who make an effort to use their language.

- **Understand Hospitality Norms:** Egyptians are famously hospitable. If invited to someone's home, it's polite to bring a small gift like sweets or dates. Also, accepting tea or coffee is a sign of respect. Be ready for offers of food and conversation—it's part of the culture.

- **Use Your Right Hand:** When handing over money, gifts, or eating, use your right hand or both hands, as the left hand is considered unclean in Egyptian culture.

- **Be Patient and Flexible:** Daily life in Egypt can be more relaxed about time and schedules. Showing patience, smiling, and going with the flow can make your experience much smoother and more enjoyable.

# CRIME IN EGYPT

- Overview
- Crime Hotspots in Egypt
- Crime Statistics
- Quick Safety Tips

# CRIME IN EGYPT

## Overview

Egypt is **generally considered a safe country for travelers**, particularly in major tourist destinations like Cairo, Luxor, and Sharm El-Sheikh. Over recent years, crime rates in Egypt have been on a **downward trend**. Current data, such as from Numbeo's 2025 Crime Index, places Egypt at a **moderate crime level** compared to other countries, with a crime index of approximately 47.3.[2] Theft rates have also decreased significantly over the past decade, and improvements in crime detection rates have been reported.

Several factors contribute to crime in Egypt. Economic challenges like **high unemployment** and **poverty** can lead some individuals toward criminal activity. **Corruption** remains an issue, with enforcement often inconsistent, which can foster impunity in certain sectors. Additionally, Egypt faces **challenges with human trafficking**, especially affecting women and children who are vulnerable to forced labor and exploitation.

Travelers are advised to stay informed about local conditions, avoid isolated areas after dark, secure their belongings to prevent petty theft, and respect local customs and laws to reduce risks.

---

2    https://www.numbeo.com/crime/rankings_by_country.jsp

## Crime Hotspots in Egypt

In Egypt, crime hotspots are primarily found in **specific urban areas**, with some neighborhoods in Cairo and Alexandria experiencing higher levels of petty crime. In **Cairo**, areas such as **parts of downtown, neighborhoods around Ramses Square**, and certain **outskirts** away from main tourist routes have seen more incidents of pickpocketing, purse snatching, and scams targeting both locals and tourists. These crimes often occur in crowded markets, busy streets, and on public transportation. Alexandria, Egypt's second-largest city, shows similar patterns, with crowded markets and public transit areas being common places for petty theft. However, popular tourist sites like the Giza Plateau, where the pyramids are located, generally have a strong security presence, reducing the risk of crime for visitors in those zones.

When comparing Egypt to the United States, Egypt's rates of violent crimes such as homicide and armed robbery are typically lower. However, petty theft and tourist-targeted scams can be more frequent in Egypt's busy urban areas. Travelers should be particularly cautious in crowded settings and avoid displaying valuables openly. The U.S. Department of State currently rates Egypt as mostly safe for tourists who take standard precautions but advises extra caution in regions like the Sinai Peninsula due to ongoing security concerns involving militant groups.

 For those planning travel, the **U.S. Department of State travel advisory** page (**travel.state.gov**) provides the most current information about safety risks by region.

## Crime Statistics

In Egypt, the most common crimes are non-violent and opportunistic: **petty theft** (pickpocketing, bag snatching, phone snatching), **scams** (fake guides, taxi overcharging, counterfeit goods), and **street harassment** (especially targeting women, including unwanted touching and catcalling). According to Numbeo, about 5.3% of the population is affected by petty theft annually, and around 8.3% experience theft from vehicles;

violent crime rates such as assault (~0.2%) and robbery (~0.9%) remain low. Cybercrime, drug trafficking fraud, and human trafficking are also concerns.

**Law enforcement in Egypt faces serious challenges.** Corruption and lack of accountability are widespread: police often arrive late, fail to prevent or properly investigate crimes, and sometimes demand bribes or engage in harassment themselves . The judiciary is also seen as politicized and undertrained, which hinders effective crime prevention and enforcement Public trust remains low, with many believing that petty corruption undermines overall safety.

Tourists in Egypt are especially vulnerable to **petty theft**, **scams**, and **street harassment**—particularly women, who report pervasive sexual harassment in public. Violent crimes against tourists are rare but do occur, such as opportunistic attacks, occasionally including stabbings or armed hold-ups, with tourist buses and hotels sometimes targeted by militant activity.

 **Quick Safety Tips**

- Stay alert in crowded places like markets and metro stations to avoid pickpocketing and bag snatching.

- Keep valuables secure and avoid displaying expensive items like jewelry or large amounts of cash.

- Use reputable transportation such as registered taxis or ride-hailing apps like Uber or Careem.

- Avoid accepting unsolicited help or tours from strangers.

- Stick to well-lit, busy areas at night and avoid unfamiliar neighborhoods.

- Keep photocopies of your passport, visa, and important documents in a separate place from the originals.

- Save emergency contact numbers, including your embassy or consulate, in case of theft or loss.

# CRIMINAL LAW VIOLATIONS

## IN THIS CHAPTER

- Marijuana and Other Drugs in Egypt
- Penalties
- Prescription Medication
- General Questions
- Law of the Land Hypothetical
- Takeaways

## CHAPTER 4
# CRIMINAL LAW VIOLATIONS

## Marijuana and Other Drugs in Egypt

Cannabis has a long historical presence in Egypt, dating back to ancient times when it was used for medicinal and spiritual purposes. During the Islamic era, especially under the Mamluks, hashish became widely used despite religious bans, and this continued into modern times. The British colonial administration in the 19th and early 20th centuries enforced stricter prohibitions, laying the groundwork for current drug laws.

There is **no legal distinction between medical and recreational marijuana** in Egypt. Both are **strictly illegal**, and the government does not permit medical marijuana use under any circumstances. Although some people claim therapeutic benefits from cannabis, there is no regulatory framework allowing its use for health purposes, and doing so can result in criminal prosecution. **Synthetic cannabinoids** such as Spice and K2 are **also illegal** in Egypt. In response to their increasing use and the difficulty of detection, Egyptian lawmakers passed legislation in 2020 to criminalize synthetic drugs comprehensively. The law grants authorities the power to prosecute new substances not previously listed in older drug schedules by banning any compound with similar effects.

Cannabis remains illegal under Egypt's **Anti-Narcotics Law No. 182 of 1960**, which has been amended over the years to tighten drug regulations. The law criminalizes possession, use, production, and trafficking.

Possession of even small amounts can result in several years in prison, while large-scale trafficking can lead to life sentences or in extreme cases even the death penalty. While marijuana is officially illegal in Egypt and punishable under harsh drug laws, enforcement can be inconsistent, particularly when it comes to small-scale personal use. In some areas, especially in less conservative or tourist-frequented regions, authorities may overlook minor infractions or issue informal warnings rather than pursuing formal charges. However, this leniency is not guaranteed and should not be relied upon, as enforcement varies by region, circumstance, and the discretion of individual officers.

There are **no legal allowances or exceptions for marijuana use** in Egypt. All use—whether recreational, medicinal, or religious—is prohibited. **Tourists are subject to the same laws as locals**, and being found with drugs at airports, hotels, or checkpoints can result in immediate arrest and lengthy imprisonment. Even being under the influence is grounds for legal action.

Drug laws in Egypt cover a wide array of substances beyond cannabis, including **heroin, cocaine, amphetamines**, and **prescription medications** that are not declared or legally prescribed. The country imposes harsh sentences for drug offenses. Possession with intent to distribute and trafficking offenses are especially punished, and capital punishment remains a legal penalty for serious drug crimes.

## Penalties

The amended Law No. 182 of 1960 outlines a tiered system of penalties based on the nature of the offense—ranging from personal possession to trafficking and cultivation. For simple **possession for personal use**, the penalties typically include a **minimum of one to five years in prison** and **fines up to 10,000 Egyptian pounds (approximately $210 to $320 USD)**. However, sentencing can be influenced by factors such as prior criminal history, the quantity of cannabis found, and the specific circumstances of the arrest. First-time offenders in possession of small amounts may receive more lenient treatment in practice, especially in informal or negotiated settings, but the legal risk remains substantial.

Those charged with **possession with intent to distribute** face much harsher consequences, often starting at **life imprisonment**, and in particularly severe cases, such as high-volume trafficking or repeat offenses, the law allows for the **death penalty**. Egypt has sentenced individuals to death for drug-related crimes, including marijuana trafficking, although executions for cannabis are rare and usually associated with broader smuggling networks.

**Cultivating cannabis plants** is explicitly prohibited and punishable by a **minimum of five years' imprisonment** and heavy fines. If the cultivation is linked to trafficking or large-scale distribution, penalties escalate accordingly.

Egyptian drug laws also apply to **foreign nationals**, who are subject to the same punishments as citizens. Although consular assistance is available, embassies typically cannot intervene in legal proceedings. Foreigners found guilty may be **deported** after serving their sentence and **banned from re-entry**. As mentioned before, despite the severity of the laws, actual enforcement can vary. Some urban or tourist-heavy areas are known for informal leniency toward minor possession cases, with reports of bribes or informal warnings in lieu of arrest. However, this is not guaranteed and relying on such inconsistencies can result in serious legal jeopardy.

## Prescription Medication

Bringing prescription or over-the-counter (OTC) medications into Egypt is subject to strict regulations, and failure to comply can result in serious legal consequences. Travelers are allowed to bring **personal-use quantities of prescription medication**, but they must carry an **official prescription** issued by a licensed medical provider. The prescription should clearly state the traveler's name, the medication name, dosage, and the prescribing doctor's contact details. It is strongly advised to carry medications **in original, labeled packaging**, and to bring a **translated copy of the prescription in Arabic if possible**.

Certain medications that are legal in other countries may be classified as controlled substances in Egypt, including drugs containing **tramadol, codeine, pregabalin** (Lyrica), and **some sleep aids or anti-anxiety medications**. These are considered narcotics under Egyptian law, and possession without specific prior authorization or clear documentation can result in **arrest, confiscation of the drugs, fines**, or even **imprisonment**.

Over-the-counter medications are generally permitted if brought in small quantities for personal use, but **medications containing ingredients such as pseudoephedrine or codeine** (commonly found in cough syrups or cold remedies) may be **restricted or outright prohibited**.

Travelers found carrying restricted medications without proper documentation may face **criminal charges, detention**, and **possible court proceedings**. Egypt does not treat drug-related violations lightly, even when medications are legally prescribed in the traveler's home country.

For a safe visit, travelers should consult the Egyptian embassy or consulate before departure to verify the status of specific medications and are advised to carry a doctor's letter as an added precaution.

 **General Questions**

1. *Is cannabis legal in Egypt?* **No.** Cannabis is **not legal in Egypt.** It is banned under Law No. 182 of 1960, with strict penalties for possession, use, cultivation, or trafficking. Punishments range from prison sentences and fines to life imprisonment or even the death penalty for large-scale trafficking. There is **no allowance for medical use**, and while enforcement may be more relaxed in some areas for personal use, this is unpredictable and still carries legal risk.

2. *Can I legally purchase marijuana anywhere in Egypt?* **No.**
   You cannot legally purchase marijuana anywhere in Egypt. All
   forms of cannabis are illegal, and there are **no licensed dis-
   pensaries or legal markets** for medical or recreational use.
   Buying, selling, or even attempting to purchase marijuana can
   result in arrest, prosecution, and severe penalties, including
   imprisonment.

3. *Can I have marijuana on my person or in hotel room in
   Egypt?* **No.** You **cannot legally possess marijuana** in Egypt—
   whether on your person, in a hotel room, or anywhere else.
   Possession of any amount is considered a criminal offense under
   Egyptian law, even if the marijuana is for personal use. Hotels
   do not offer protection from prosecution, and staff are legally
   required to report drug-related activity.

4. *Are there any other exceptions to the possession and consumption of cannabis in Egypt?* **No. There are no exceptions** to the
   possession and consumption of cannabis in Egypt. It is strictly
   illegal for any purpose, including medical use or CBD products,
   and penalties can be severe.

5. *What are the penalties for possessing and consuming other
   types of illicit drugs in Egypt?* Egypt imposes strict penalties
   for illicit drug possession and use, including imprisonment and
   heavy fines. Fines range from 50,000 to 300,000 EGP (about
   $1,600 to $9,600 USD), depending on the offense. Drug trafficking can lead to life imprisonment or the death penalty. Even
   unintentional possession can result in fines and jail time. These
   laws apply equally to both locals and foreigners, and enforcement
   is rigorous.

## Law of the Land Hypothetical

HYPOTHETICAL: *Sarah, a tourist visiting Egypt, carries a small amount of cannabis in her luggage, intending to use it during her stay to manage chronic pain. She also brings a prescription pain medication from her home country, but does not have a copy of the prescription or any official documentation. What legal risks does Sarah face under Egyptian law for possessing cannabis and undeclared prescription medication, and what are the potential penalties?*

ANSWER: *Under Egyptian law, Sarah faces serious legal risks. Cannabis possession is strictly illegal in Egypt with no exceptions, including for medical use. Additionally, bringing prescription medication without proper documentation, especially if it contains controlled substances like certain painkillers, can result in arrest, confiscation of the drugs, fines, and imprisonment. Sarah could be charged with drug possession and possibly trafficking depending on the quantity and circumstances. Foreign nationals are subject to the same laws and penalties as citizens, so Sarah's status as a tourist does not provide any protection. She may face imprisonment and fines and could be deported after serving any sentence. It is critical for travelers to carry official prescriptions and declare all medications to avoid such legal consequences in Egypt.*

## Takeaways

- Cannabis is strictly illegal in Egypt with no legal distinction between medical or recreational use, and no exceptions for possession, consumption, or cultivation.

- Penalties for drug offenses are severe, ranging from imprisonment and heavy fines to life sentences and the death penalty for trafficking.

- Prescription and over-the-counter medications are tightly regulated; travelers must carry proper documentation to avoid legal trouble, especially for controlled substances like tramadol or codeine.

- Foreigners are subject to the same drug laws and penalties as Egyptian citizens, with potential deportation after serving sentences.

- Enforcement can be inconsistent, particularly for minor cannabis possession in some areas, but relying on leniency is risky and can lead to serious legal consequences.

# ALCOHOL-RELATED OFFENSES

# ALCOHOL-RELATED OFFENSES

## Alcohol-Related Offenses[3]

Alcohol has a complex history in Egypt. Ancient Egyptians brewed beer and made wine thousands of years ago, integrating these drinks into religious rituals and daily life. Over centuries, especially with the rise of Islam as the dominant religion, attitudes toward alcohol became more restrictive, as Islamic teachings generally prohibit its consumption. Despite religious discouragement, alcohol has remained part of social and cultural life for many Egyptians, especially among non-Muslim communities and in cosmopolitan urban centers.

Alcohol is not a central part of daily life for most Egyptians, particularly the Muslim majority, who often abstain for religious reasons. However, it is consumed socially in some circles, including by Christian minorities, expatriates, tourists, and some secular Egyptians. Drinking is more common in major cities like Cairo and Alexandria, in licensed venues such as bars, restaurants, and hotels catering to locals and visitors alike. Alcohol consumption is generally more discreet in public due to cultural sensitivities and legal restrictions.

Traditional Egyptian alcoholic beverages include local beers and wines. **Beer** brands like **Stella** and **Sakara** are popular domestic options, while local wine production exists but is less prominent internationally.

---

3   https://travel2egypt.org/alcohol-in-egypt/

Imported liquors such as whiskey, vodka, and brandy are also available in licensed outlets. Additionally, some traditional fermented beverages from rural areas may have low alcohol content but are less widely consumed.

**Alcohol is legal in Egypt but heavily regulated.** It can only be sold and consumed in licensed establishments such as hotels, bars, clubs, and certain restaurants. Retail sales are restricted to licensed stores, and public consumption is prohibited. The **legal drinking age is 21.** Selling alcohol without a license or drinking in public places can lead to fines, arrest, or other penalties. Though alcohol is available, it is less accessible than in many Western countries, reflecting cultural norms and religious influences. Tourist areas and major urban centers offer more options for purchasing and consuming alcohol legally.

## Alcohol Regulation

While legal, alcohol in Egypt is governed by strict regulations that reflect both the country's Islamic cultural foundations and its secular legal framework. While tourists and non-Muslim residents can purchase and consume alcohol, access is limited to licensed venues such as hotels, bars, select restaurants, and government-authorized liquor stores. **Public consumption is prohibited**, and drinking in streets or parks can result in fines or even short jail sentences.

The **legal drinking age** in Egypt is **21.** Enforcement of alcohol laws can vary by region; for example, in tourist hubs like Sharm El Sheikh or certain areas of Cairo, alcohol consumption is more tolerated and widely available. However, in more conservative or rural areas, access may be extremely limited, and cultural disapproval more pronounced.

Licensed sellers and venues must strictly follow government guidelines. Selling or serving alcohol without a license is illegal and can result in **hefty fines** and **more than a year in prison.** Venues found in violation can also be shut down temporarily or permanently. During religious periods such as Ramadan, the sale of alcohol to Egyptian citizens is typically banned, though licensed establishments catering to foreigners may continue serving non-Muslim guests. Additionally, advertising alcohol is completely prohibited, and driving under the influence is treated seriously. Egypt enforces a low legal blood alcohol limit of **0.05%**, and penalties for drunk driving can include fines, imprisonment, and license suspension.

Although alcohol is available, it is **heavily taxed**—often marked up by 2,500–3,000%—making it expensive by international standards. In some cases, patrons may bring their own alcohol to non-licensed venues for a corkage fee, though this practice is not formally regulated.

## Things to Remember

- **Drinking Age:** The legal drinking age in Egypt is **21** for both locals and tourists.

- **ID:** ID is typically required to purchase alcohol in licensed venues or stores, especially in hotels or duty-free shops. Passports or government-issued IDs are commonly accepted.

- **Public Consumption: Illegal**. Drinking alcohol in public places such as streets, parks, or beaches is prohibited. Violators can face fines or brief detention.

- **Public Drunkenness:** Public intoxication can result in arrest, fines up to 200 EGP (around $6 USD), and possibly a short jail term. Enforcement varies but is generally stricter outside tourist zones.

- **Drunk Driving:** The legal blood alcohol limit is **0.05%**. Penalties for violating this include fines, imprisonment, license suspension, and vehicle confiscation.

- **Purchase of Alcohol:** Alcohol is **legally sold** in licensed hotels, restaurants, bars, and government-approved liquor stores. It is banned during Ramadan for Egyptian citizens, though foreigners may still be served in tourist establishments. Alcohol cannot be sold without a license.

- **Alcohol Permits:** There is no formal system for alcohol permits for private events, but only licensed venues can legally serve alcohol. Hosting events with alcohol in unlicensed spaces may attract legal issues if authorities intervene.

- **Illegal Alcohol:** Illegal or counterfeit alcohol is **a concern in some unregulated areas** and can pose serious health risks. Always purchase alcohol from licensed and reputable vendors to avoid dangerous or toxic substances.

 **General Questions**

1. *Can I drink and drive in Egypt?* **No.** You cannot legally drink and drive in Egypt. The legal blood alcohol limit is **0.05%**, and driving under the influence is strictly prohibited. Penalties can include fines, imprisonment, license suspension, and vehicle confiscation. Enforcement may be especially strict in the event of accidents or checkpoints.

2. *Can I possess an open container in public?* **No.** You cannot legally possess an open container in public in Egypt. Public drinking is prohibited and can result in fines, arrest, or detention—even in tourist areas where enforcement may be more relaxed.

 **Law of the Land Hypothetical**

HYPOTHETICAL: *Mark, a tourist visiting Cairo, buys a bottle of alcohol from a licensed liquor store to take back to his hotel. On his way, he is stopped by police while walking in a public park with the unopened bottle in hand.*

*Is Mark allowed to carry unopened alcohol in public places like parks, and could he face any penalties?*

**ANSWER:** *Carrying unopened alcohol in public places like parks is generally frowned upon in Egypt, and public consumption is strictly prohibited. While the bottle is unopened, walking with it openly in public may attract police attention. Although laws focus mainly on open containers and public drinking, Mark could still face questioning, fines, or warnings for displaying alcohol publicly, especially outside licensed venues. Tourists are advised to keep alcohol consumption within licensed hotels or bars and avoid carrying alcohol openly in public areas to prevent legal issues.*

 **Takeaways**

- Alcohol is legal in Egypt but strictly regulated, available only in licensed venues like hotels, bars, and government-approved stores.

- The legal drinking age is **21**, and public consumption—including carrying open containers—is prohibited and punishable by fines or detention.

- Drinking during Ramadan is banned for Egyptian citizens, though tourists may still be served alcohol in licensed tourist establishments.

- Driving under the influence is illegal with a blood alcohol limit of **0.05%**; penalties include fines, imprisonment, and license suspension.

- Illegal or counterfeit alcohol is a health risk, so purchasing alcohol only from licensed and reputable sources is essential.

# FIREARM & AMMUNITION OFFENSES

## CHAPTER 6

# FIREARM & AMMUNITION OFFENSES

## Current Firearm Status and Related Penalties[4]

Egyptian citizens **may legally own firearms**, but the process is stringent. Applicants must submit a request to the local police, undergo a background check, provide a valid reason for ownership (such as self-defense or hunting), complete a firearm safety course, and pass both written and practical exams. Approval from the Ministry of Interior is required, and licenses must be renewed every three years. Foreigners residing in Egypt, on the other hand, are **generally prohibited from owning firearms**, except for specific cases like hunting, which require special permission from the Ministry of Interior.

Possessing an unlicensed firearm in Egypt is a serious offense. Penalties vary based on the type of weapon:

- **Shotguns and similar firearms:** Punishable by imprisonment and a fine up to 5,000 EGP (approximately $320 USD).
- **Pistols and rifled-barrel guns:** Punishable by a fine up to 15,000 EGP (approximately $960 USD) and hard labor.

---

4    https://gunpolicy.org/firearms/citation/quotes

- **Machine guns, automatic rifles, and explosives:** Punishable by life imprisonment with hard labor and a fine up to 20,000 EGP (approximately $1,280 USD).

Additionally, acquiring or possessing firearms in public places or with intent to undermine public order can lead to **life imprisonment or even the death penalty.**[5]

While the laws are strict, enforcement can be inconsistent, particularly in urban areas. The proliferation of unlicensed firearms, often due to smuggling and theft, poses challenges to law enforcement. Authorities have initiated programs to confiscate illegal weapons and encourage voluntary surrender.

Public opinion on firearms in Egypt is divided. Some view firearms as essential for self-defense, while others consider them a threat to public safety. The government maintains a strong stance on gun control, citing concerns about terrorism and civil unrest.

 **Penalties**

Firearm-related penalties in Egypt are severe, with laws designed to strictly limit civilian access to weapons. Possessing an unlicensed shotgun or smooth-bore firearm is punishable by imprisonment and a fine of up to **5,000 EGP (about $98 USD)**. Possession of pistols or rifled-barrel firearms carries harsher consequences, including hard labor and fines of up to **15,000 EGP (around $295 USD)**. For automatic weapons, machine guns, or explosives, the penalty is life imprisonment with hard labor and a fine of up to **20,000 EGP (about $395 USD)**.

---

5   gunpolicy.org

Carrying a firearm in public spaces or with the intent to threaten public security can lead to life imprisonment, and in extreme cases—such as when a weapon is used to undermine public order—the death penalty may apply. Manufacturing, selling, or repairing firearms without a license is also illegal. For shotguns, this offense can result in fines between **500 and 1,000 EGP ($10 to $20 USD)** and imprisonment. The same actions involving pistols or more advanced firearms can result in hard labor and significantly longer prison terms.

Possession of ammunition without a valid permit is treated similarly, with penalties ranging from fines up to **5,000 EGP ($98 USD)** to **life imprisonment and a 20,000 EGP fine ($395 USD)** for repeat offenders or those caught with large quantities. Prior convictions or evidence of trafficking can significantly increase the severity of sentencing.

Even though these penalties don't seem significant by Western standards, they are considered **extremely high by Egyptian standards**. A fine of 5,000 to 20,000 EGP can equal one to three months' wages for the average Egyptian worker, whose monthly income typically ranges from 7,000 to 9,000 EGP (about $140 to $180 USD). For many, even the lower-end fines are financially burdensome. Additionally, the application of **life imprisonment with hard labor**—and in some cases the **death penalty**—reflects how serious the Egyptian government considers unauthorized firearm possession. Compared to penalties for other crimes, those for firearms are among the most severe in the country, designed to deter illicit weapon ownership and respond to threats related to public safety, terrorism, and political unrest.

## Firearm Restrictions for Visitors

Visitors and non-citizens are **strictly prohibited** from bringing firearms into Egypt. Egyptian law does not grant tourists or foreign residents the right to possess, carry, or transport firearms or ammunition under any circumstances, even if the weapon is legally owned in their home country. There is **no legal reciprocity** for foreign gun licenses, and **no exemptions** for self-defense, hunting, or sport shooting without **explicit prior authorization** from the Egyptian Ministry of Interior—which is extremely rare and typically reserved for diplomatic or official purposes. Bringing a firearm into Egypt—whether intentionally or unknowingly—can result in **immediate arrest, prosecution,** and **severe penalties,** including fines, imprisonment, or even **life sentences** for certain categories of weapons. After serving a sentence, foreign nationals are often deported and may be banned from re-entering the country.

Customs inspections at airports and borders are thorough, and Egyptian authorities maintain a **zero-tolerance policy** for firearm violations by foreigners. Tourists are strongly advised **not to carry any weapon or ammunition,** including items stored in checked luggage, as even accidental possession can trigger serious legal consequences.

 **General Questions**

1. *What happens if the police catch me carrying a firearm in Egypt?* If police catch you carrying a firearm in Egypt without a valid license, you will be arrested and face severe penalties. Depending on the weapon, fines can range from about 5,000 EGP ($98 USD) to 20,000 EGP ($395 USD), with possible imprisonment, hard labor, or even life sentences for serious offenses. Carrying a firearm in public or threatening public safety can lead to harsher punishments, including the death penalty in extreme cases. Foreigners face the same penalties as Egyptians and may also be deported and banned from re-entry after serving any sentence. Enforcement is strict, and even accidental possession carries serious risks.

2. ***Can tourists bring hunting or sporting firearms into Egypt with special permits?*** **No**. Tourists cannot legally bring hunting or sporting firearms into Egypt, even with special permits. Egypt has a strict zero-tolerance policy on firearm imports for non-citizens and does not recognize foreign firearm licenses. Attempting to bring firearms can lead to imprisonment, fines, and deportation. Visitors should leave guns at home and consider renting equipment locally if needed.

 **Law of the Land Hypothetical**

HYPOTHETICAL: *John, a British tourist visiting Egypt, carries a small pistol in his suitcase, believing his valid UK firearm license allows him to bring it legally. At customs in Cairo, officials discover the pistol during an X-ray inspection and detain him immediately. Can John legally bring his licensed pistol into Egypt, and what penalties could he face for unauthorized possession?*

ANSWER: *No. Egypt does not recognize foreign firearm licenses, and tourists are strictly prohibited from bringing any firearms or ammunition into the country without prior approval from the Egyptian Ministry of Interior—a permission rarely granted. John's possession of the pistol without this authorization is illegal. He faces serious charges that can include imprisonment, fines up to 20,000 EGP (approximately $395 USD), and possibly hard labor. After legal proceedings, he may also be deported and banned from re-entering Egypt. Tourists should never carry firearms when traveling to Egypt to avoid such severe penalties.*

 **Takeaways**

- Egyptian citizens may legally own firearms, but the licensing process is strict, requiring background checks, safety courses, exams, and government approval. Foreigners generally cannot own firearms without special permission, which is rarely granted.

- Possessing unlicensed firearms carries severe penalties that vary by weapon type—from fines around 5,000 EGP (about $98 USD) and imprisonment for shotguns, up to life imprisonment with hard labor and fines up to 20,000 EGP (about $395 USD) for automatic weapons or explosives. Carrying guns in public or threatening public security can lead to life sentences or the death penalty.

- Although harsh by Egyptian standards, with fines representing one to three months' wages for many, enforcement can be inconsistent. The government remains strict due to concerns about terrorism, civil unrest, and public safety.

- Egyptian public opinion on firearms is mixed—while some people see guns as necessary for self-defense, many view them as a threat to public safety. This division influences how firearm laws are enforced and reflects broader concerns about security, terrorism, and social stability in the country.

CHAPTER 7

# PROSTITUTION

# PROSTITUTION

## Overview

Prostitution is **illegal** in Egypt and is considered both a **criminal offense and a violation of public morality**. The country's legal system, influenced by Islamic values and conservative social norms, treats prostitution harshly, whether it involves Egyptian citizens or foreign nationals. While prostitution does occur in underground networks, Egyptian authorities enforce strict penalties for those involved in any aspect of it, from solicitation and brothel-keeping to human trafficking. These laws are outlined in several criminal provisions, including Law No. 10 of 1961, which targets acts of debauchery and the promotion of prostitution. Violations can lead to arrest, fines, imprisonment, and in the case of foreign visitors, deportation following prosecution.

Enforcement of these laws is not limited to overt criminal activity. Egyptian police have been known to carry out sting operations, particularly in major cities like Cairo, Alexandria, and tourist hotspots near the Red Sea. Undercover officers sometimes pose as clients or providers to catch individuals in the act. Even private arrangements, such as those made on dating apps or via social media, may be monitored under Egypt's cybercrime laws, which allow authorities to interpret a wide range of online behavior as promotion of immoral acts. This means that travelers who believe they are engaging in consensual, private interactions may still find themselves on the wrong side of the law.

Many foreign visitors mistakenly assume that what may be tolerated or overlooked in resort areas is somehow legal. In reality, **laws apply across the country**, and their enforcement can be unpredictable but severe. There have been cases where hotel staff have reported foreign guests for inviting Egyptians of the opposite sex to their rooms, particularly when they lacked a marriage certificate. Even the appearance of impropriety, in the eyes of authorities or hotel management, can result in police involvement. These actions are often justified under the broad umbrella of protecting public morality.

One high-profile example occurred in 2021, when several young Egyptian women on TikTok were arrested and sentenced to prison for allegedly violating public decency. While none were accused of actual prostitution, prosecutors framed their social media content as immoral, citing it as harmful to traditional family values. This reflects the broad and often subjective interpretation of moral violations under Egyptian law, and highlights how even indirect behavior—especially when amplified online—can be criminalized.

For travelers, the safest course of action is to **avoid any engagement**, real or implied, in the sex trade or in behavior that could be seen as suggestive or inappropriate by local standards. This includes avoiding solicitation, refraining from suggestive discussions or content on social media, and being cautious when using dating apps. What might seem like harmless fun in one country could carry serious legal consequences in Egypt. If ever approached by law enforcement, it is crucial to remain calm, request contact with your embassy or consulate, and avoid signing any documents without legal representation or a qualified translator.[6]

## Laws and Penalties

Prostitution in Egypt is illegal and **unregulated in any official capacity**. There are no legalized red-light districts, no government oversight of sex work, and no legal framework for the licensing, registration, or

---

6    https://www.theguardian.com/world/2021/jan/12/
     egyptian-court-acquits-women-jailed-for-inciting-debauchery-on-tiktok

protection of individuals involved in the sex trade. Instead, the state treats prostitution as a criminal offense under public morality and vice laws, with no distinction between consensual commercial sex work and other forms of sexual exploitation.

Egyptian law prohibits not only the act of prostitution itself but also a wide range of related activities. These include **solicitation, brothel operation, pimping, living off the earnings of prostitution, and inciting or facilitating debauchery**. Law No. 10 of 1961 on the Combat of Prostitution serves as the primary legal instrument in this area, and it is enforced with the backing of both civil authorities and moral policing units. While there is no formal designation of zones where prostitution is tolerated, some areas in Cairo and tourist-heavy neighborhoods have gained reputations for illicit activity. However, these are not sanctioned by the state, and police regularly conduct raids and surveillance operations in such locations.

Sex workers are not afforded legal rights or protections under Egyptian law. There are no health or licensing requirements, no labor protections, and no official acknowledgment of sex work as a form of employment. In fact, identifying oneself as a sex worker can lead directly to arrest and prosecution. Police often target women based on vague allegations of "debauchery" or "immoral conduct," and evidence can include online communications, lifestyle choices, or simply being in a hotel room with a person of the opposite sex without marital documentation.

Penalties for prostitution-related offenses vary depending on the charges. Individuals found guilty of offering or engaging in prostitution can face **imprisonment** ranging from **three months to three years**. Those convicted of more serious charges, such as operating a brothel or trafficking in persons, can receive sentences of **five years or more**. Repeat offenders and those involved in organized prostitution networks face harsher penalties. In addition to incarceration, convicted foreigners may be **deported** after serving their sentence. Public exposure and social stigma are often part of the fallout, with cases sometimes publicized in local media or online forums.

In short, Egypt treats prostitution as a criminal and moral issue rather than a matter of public health or human rights. There are no legal pathways for sex work, no regulated zones of tolerance, and little leniency for those caught in the system. Travelers should be aware that even indirect association with prostitution—such as messaging someone online who turns out to be under surveillance—can result in serious legal consequences.

## Prostitution Practices

In Egypt, reliable data on prostitution is scarce, however one study found that around 39% of women identified sex work as their only source of income, alongside roles like hostess, housemaid, or dancer. Most rely on street solicitation (28%), intermediaries (22%), or bars (20%) to find clients.[7]

Although prostitution is illegal, it nonetheless manifests in multiple forms. **Street-based sex work** in urban centers remains common, with sex workers often working alone or through informal pimps known locally as "networks," particularly in Cairo and Alexandria. **Brothels** exist underground, as do **escort services** that cater to wealthier Egyptians, Gulf tourists, or even foreigners. Some refer to "escort" or "bar hostesses" who provide companionship—sometimes sexual—via **intermediaries**, though law enforcement often equates these arrangements with prostitution. Temporary or "summer marriages" arranged between tourists—often from Gulf countries—and locals sometimes serve as a means to circumvent laws, though they can easily evolve into exploitative or trafficked situations.

**Online platforms** have become another arena for sex work, despite mounting enforcement. The 2018 Cybercrime Law broadened the definition of "debauchery" to include digital expressions that conflict with "family values and social tradition". Authorities use dating apps and social media to entrap individuals, and "invitations" to sexual

---

7    https://en.wikipedia.org/wiki/Prostitution_in_Egypt

encounters—especially online—may be prosecuted as moral offenses, even without physical solicitation.

Local authorities take a highly punitive stance toward all forms of prostitution. Police conduct street sweeps, operate undercover stings, and close venues suspected of commercial sex. The penal system under Law 10/1961 applies equally to street work, brothels, pimping, and online facilitation. Beyond criminal penalties, public morality divisions and cybercrime units clamp down on perceived threats to social order. Sex workers have no official protections, no access to healthcare or rights as laborers, and are frequently stigmatized or criminalized—even when they are victims of trafficking. In many cases, trafficking survivors are prosecuted alongside offenders rather than recognized as victims, highlighting the state's morally driven enforcement approach.

## Sex Trafficking and Exploitation

Sex trafficking and sexual exploitation remain **serious concerns** in Egypt. The country functions both as a source and destination for trafficking, with vulnerabilities rooted in economic hardship, displacement, and weak enforcement mechanisms. Although exact numbers are difficult to verify, international organizations and local reports consistently indicate that sex trafficking affects thousands, particularly women and children, across both urban and rural areas. Girls from impoverished communities are often targeted for what are known as **"summer marriages,"** in which wealthy foreign men—typically from Gulf countries—enter temporary marital arrangements with young Egyptian girls. These arrangements, often brokered by families or middlemen, are a form of legalized exploitation that disguises sex trafficking behind a culturally acceptable framework.

Major cities like **Cairo**, **Alexandria**, and **Giza**, as well as tourist-heavy areas such as **Luxor** and **Sharm El-Sheikh**, have been flagged as **high-risk zones** where trafficking networks operate with relative ease. In addition to domestic victims, foreign nationals—especially migrants and refugees from sub-Saharan Africa, Southeast Asia, and the Horn of Africa—are frequently subjected to forced prostitution. Many of these individuals are smuggled into the country with the promise of work, only to be coerced into sex work under threat of violence, debt, or deportation. Egypt's geographic location also places it along migratory routes used by smugglers, making it both a transit and destination country for trafficked persons.

The demographic most at risk includes **poor Egyptian children**, particularly girls, as well as **unaccompanied migrant women** and **undocumented domestic workers**. **Refugees**, especially those from Eritrea, Sudan, and Ethiopia, are extremely vulnerable to exploitation, with many women reporting cases of sexual abuse in detention centers, private homes, and informal workplaces. Despite the gravity of the situation, many victims are either unaware of their rights or too fearful to seek help. In some cases, those who do report abuse are treated as criminals, charged with prostitution or immigration violations, rather than recognized as trafficking survivors.

The Egyptian government has made some attempts to confront the problem. **Law No. 64 of 2010** criminalizes all forms of human trafficking, including sexual exploitation. National anti-trafficking strategies have been introduced, most recently a 2022–2026 action plan that includes public awareness campaigns, expanded shelters for women, and increased cooperation between ministries.[8] Egypt has also prosecuted traffickers in recent years, with some success in convicting individuals involved in sex trafficking. However, challenges persist. Identification of victims remains inconsistent, law enforcement officers are not always trained in trauma-informed practices, and shelters—especially for foreign nationals or men—are limited. Often, victims are detained or deported before they can access assistance.

Despite official efforts, many international observers, including the U.S. State Department, continue to rank Egypt as a country that falls short of fully meeting the standards necessary to combat trafficking effectively. While the laws are on the books, enforcement is uneven, and systemic obstacles such as corruption, lack of resources, and entrenched social attitudes hinder meaningful progress. For travelers, this reality

---

8    https://www.ecoi.net/en/document/2093657.html

underscores the importance of vigilance, especially in interactions that may inadvertently involve exploitative arrangements. Understanding the broader context of trafficking in Egypt not only helps protect vulnerable individuals but also ensures that visitors do not unknowingly support systems of abuse.

 ## Sex Tourism and Public Health

Sex tourism in Egypt exists, but it **operates covertly** due to the country's strict laws and conservative cultural norms. While not openly acknowledged or organized in any official capacity, informal networks catering to sex tourism do operate, particularly in areas with high tourist traffic. These include parts of **Cairo**, **Alexandria**, and certain Red Sea resorts like **Hurghada** and **Sharm El-Sheikh**. In these areas, some individuals or networks discreetly offer sexual services to foreign visitors, often under the guise of companionship, escort services, or temporary "marriage" arrangements. These transactions may be facilitated by hotel staff, private drivers, or online platforms, but they remain illegal and risky for all parties involved.

A unique and troubling aspect of sex tourism in Egypt is the phenomenon of aforementioned "summer marriages," where older male tourists—primarily from Gulf states—enter temporary unions with underage or economically vulnerable Egyptian girls. These arrangements, often orchestrated by brokers and sanctioned by complicit families, are a socially tolerated form of sex tourism that blends cultural tradition with financial desperation. Although framed as legal marriages, they typically last only a few weeks or months, and the young brides are often left with no legal or financial protection once the tourists leave.

While there is no public advertising of sex tourism services, the internet and mobile apps have become increasingly common tools for arranging such encounters. Dating and messaging platforms are sometimes used to facilitate connections between tourists and locals willing to engage in transactional sex. However, this also places both sex workers and clients at risk of surveillance and arrest, as Egyptian authorities have been known to monitor online behavior and use entrapment tactics to target individuals suspected of violating public morality laws.

Sex tourism in Egypt raises several **public health concerns**. Because the activity is illegal and stigmatized, it occurs entirely underground, with no access to healthcare, regulation, or safe-sex education. This creates significant risks for the transmission of **sexually transmitted infections (STIs), including HIV,** particularly among vulnerable populations like underage girls and migrants. Reports suggest that condom use in such arrangements is inconsistent, and many sex workers lack access to regular medical care or testing. There is also no public health infrastructure in place to reach those engaged in transactional sex, as doing so would likely trigger legal consequences for those individuals.

In response to these risks, Egypt's public health efforts tend to focus on broader population-level health education, but do not directly address the specific needs of those involved in sex work or informal sexual economies. The absence of harm reduction strategies, coupled with harsh legal penalties, means that many cases of abuse, infection, and exploitation go unreported and untreated. For travelers, participating in or seeking out sex tourism in Egypt not only carries severe legal consequences but also contributes to a shadow economy with serious ethical and public health implications.

 ## Tips to Avoid Being Solicited

Although prostitution is illegal in Egypt, that doesn't mean travelers are immune from being approached. In some cases, solicitation may be discreet and casual; in others, it may come from someone posing as a tour guide, a hotel employee, or even a fellow traveler. While most visitors will never encounter anything of the sort, those staying in busy tourist zones—especially in Cairo, Luxor, Hurghada, and Sharm

El-Sheikh—may find themselves the target of offers that cross the line of legality.

What makes this particularly risky in Egypt is not just the act of engaging in sex work, but being associated with it in any way. Responding to a solicitation, even without following through, can lead to unwanted attention from law enforcement. In some cases, tourists have been detained or questioned simply for being in the company of someone later accused of solicitation. Online interactions carry similar risks. Dating apps and social platforms are sometimes monitored, and Egyptian police have been known to conduct sting operations or entrapment schemes using fake profiles. A friendly or flirtatious message could easily be misconstrued as immoral behavior under Egyptian vice laws.

To minimize the risk of being solicited—and avoid accidental entanglement with Egypt's strict morality laws—there are several precautions travelers should consider. First, be cautious when approached by strangers in nightlife venues, bars, or public areas, especially those who seem overly forward or vague about their intentions. Be wary of offers for private tours, massage services, or "special companionship," particularly if they come unsolicited or seem too good to be true. **Declining politely and firmly** is usually enough to deter further interaction.

When using social apps, avoid suggestive profiles, ambiguous language, or references to intimacy, even jokingly. **Keep all digital interactions clear and respectful**, and never agree to meet someone privately unless you have a legitimate, well-understood reason. In hotel settings, remember that Egyptian law requires locals and foreigners to provide proof of marriage if they share a room. Even being seen with an Egyptian national of the opposite sex in a private space can raise suspicion. Hotel staff may report interactions they find inappropriate, not out of malice, but due to legal obligations or fear of penalties themselves.

The best way to avoid problems is to understand that Egypt takes a **zero-tolerance approach to prostitution and related activities**. The enforcement may vary from one area to another, but the consequences when the law is applied can be severe—ranging from fines and detention to deportation. Knowing the social and legal landscape not only helps keep you safe, it also ensures that your time in the country is spent enjoying its rich culture, history, and hospitality—without unnecessary complications.

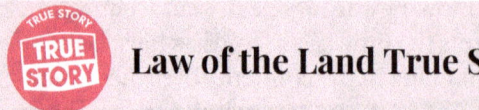 **Law of the Land True Story**[9]

In September 2023, a high-profile raid at a Giza hotel became a stark reminder of Egypt's strict stance on prostitution and public morality. Among those arrested was a well-known Egyptian belly dancer, whose performances and glamorous social media presence had earned her national recognition. That evening, vice police carried out a surprise operation based on reports of illegal activity involving the facilitation of paid sexual encounters.

Authorities alleged that several women were using hotel rooms to meet clients and that arrangements had been made discreetly through messaging apps and social media. Alongside the dancer, five other women were arrested, as well as a man accused of running an online page that promoted travel abroad for women—a page investigators believed was a front for prostitution recruitment. While no sexual acts were reportedly witnessed during the raid, prosecutors relied on digital evidence, text communications, and witness statements. The charges fell under Egypt's Law No. 10 of 1961, which criminalizes not only prostitution but also facilitation, promotion, and profit from acts deemed immoral. If convicted, those involved faced prison terms ranging from three months to several years.

The story made headlines across Egypt—not only because of the celebrity involved, but because it underscored the government's ongoing campaign against vice, both online and offline. For travelers, the implications are clear: engaging with or even being present around individuals involved in these networks can carry serious legal consequences.

---

9    https://www.world-today-news.com/
     police-arrest-famous-dancer-and-5-girls-for-prostitution-in-giza-hotel

In Egypt, mere association, even without direct involvement, can be enough to trigger detention or questioning.

This Giza case highlights how quickly an ordinary evening can turn into a legal ordeal. In a country where moral offenses are criminalized and public decency laws are enforced aggressively, even private encounters can result in very public consequences. For visitors, understanding and respecting these boundaries is not just wise—it's essential.

 **Takeaways**

- Egypt criminalizes all forms of prostitution under Law No. 10 of 1961. There are no legal red-light districts or protections for sex workers. Penalties include arrest, fines, imprisonment, and deportation for foreigners.

- Authorities monitor social media and dating apps under cyber-crime laws. Even private conversations or suggestive messages can be prosecuted as promoting debauchery. Police also use sting operations to target both locals and tourists.

- Prostitution still occurs through street work, intermediaries, or "summer marriages," especially in cities like Cairo and Sharm El-Sheikh. These activities remain illegal and risky, with no labor rights or healthcare access for those involved.

- Egypt is both a source and destination for trafficking, with women, children, and migrants most vulnerable. While anti-trafficking laws exist, enforcement is weak and victims are often treated as criminals.

- Tourists have been detained for being seen with an Egyptian of the opposite sex without a marriage certificate. In Egypt, association alone can lead to questioning or arrest. Travelers should stay aware and cautious to avoid misunderstandings.

# LGBTQ

- Homophobia in Egypt
- LGBTQ Legislation
- LGBTQ Tourism and Safety Concerns
- General Questions
- Law of the Land True Story

CHAPTER 8

# LGBTQ

## Homophobia in Egypt

Homophobia in Egypt is deeply intertwined with the country's history, culture, religion, and government policies. For many decades, Egypt's government has maintained a conservative stance toward LGBTQ+ individuals, largely shaped by prevailing cultural and religious norms. Although there is **no specific law that explicitly criminalizes homosexuality**, authorities commonly use broad and vague legal provisions related to **"debauchery," "public morality,"** and **"prostitution"** to arrest and prosecute people suspected of same-sex relations. This legal ambiguity creates an environment in which LGBTQ+ Egyptians face constant surveillance, harassment, and the threat of detention. The state's approach has been largely repressive, often marked by police raids on gatherings perceived to be LGBTQ+, entrapment through social media, and media campaigns that depict LGBTQ+ identities as threats to societal values.

The cultural attitude toward LGBTQ+ individuals in Egypt today remains **overwhelmingly negative**. Homosexuality is **widely stigmatized and socially condemned** in the mainstream. This disapproval stems in large part from the country's strong religious and social traditions. The majority of Egyptians identify as Muslim, and dominant interpretations of Islam in Egypt disapprove of same-sex relationships, framing them as morally wrong. Moreover, Egyptian society places significant emphasis on traditional family values, where family honor and social conformity are paramount. Deviations from heterosexual norms are often viewed as a direct challenge to these values, threatening the social fabric and familial bonds. This cultural conservatism means that discussions about sexuality, particularly non-heterosexual orientations, are largely taboo and rarely occur openly in public or private settings.

Homophobic attitudes manifest in everyday life in many ways. In the workplace, LGBTQ+ individuals generally feel compelled to conceal their sexual orientation to avoid discrimination or harassment, as there are no legal protections for sexual minorities. Schools can be hostile environments, where students suspected of being LGBTQ+ may face bullying or ostracism without institutional support or intervention. Within families, LGBTQ+ members risk rejection, emotional abuse, and sometimes even violence if their sexual orientation becomes known. The pressure to conform to societal expectations leads many to live secretive lives, fearing the consequences of exposure. **Publicly expressing one's LGBTQ+ identity is rare and dangerous**, as it invites both social ostracism and potential legal repercussions.

Reports of violence and discrimination against LGBTQ+ people in Egypt are widespread, although precise statistics are difficult to obtain due to the social stigma that discourages victims from reporting abuses. Human rights organizations have documented numerous instances of police raids, arbitrary arrests, and mistreatment of LGBTQ+ individuals in detention. Physical abuse, psychological torture, and degrading treatment are common experiences for those caught in the justice system on charges related to morality or indecency. These ongoing abuses contribute to an atmosphere of fear and silence that further marginalizes the community. Despite the lack of reliable official data, it is clear that LGBTQ+ Egyptians face significant and systemic violence and discrimination.

Public advocacy for LGBTQ+ rights within Egypt is **extremely limited** due to the harsh legal and social environment. There are no well-known public figures or celebrities who openly identify as LGBTQ+ or who publicly support LGBTQ+ rights. Most activists operate underground or anonymously, often relying on online platforms to connect, share information, and offer support. International human rights groups and activists in the Egyptian diaspora play an important role in raising awareness and advocating for change, but their influence within the country is constrained. The risks associated with openly promoting LGBTQ+ rights in Egypt remain substantial.

## LGBTQ Legislation

While same-sex relationships are not explicitly criminalized by a specific law, individuals suspected of engaging in homosexual acts are frequently prosecuted under broad and vague statutes related to "debauchery," "public morality," and "prostitution." These laws carry severe penalties, including **imprisonment, fines**, and in some cases, **forced medical examinations**. The legal framework is thus highly discriminatory toward LGBTQ+ individuals, effectively criminalizing their existence and behavior without directly naming homosexuality as an offense.

There are no laws in Egypt that provide any form of recognition or protection for LGBTQ+ rights. On the contrary, the country's legal system is marked by provisions that facilitate discrimination and persecution. Laws regarding public decency and morality are often weaponized to target LGBTQ+ people, and the absence of any supportive legislation leaves this community vulnerable to arbitrary arrests and mistreatment. The government's stance is therefore clearly hostile, and legal protections against discrimination on the basis of sexual orientation or gender identity do not exist.

In terms of legal protections, LGBTQ+ individuals in Egypt have **no formal safeguards** against discrimination in employment, housing, healthcare, or public services. There are no anti-discrimination statutes that include sexual orientation or gender identity, and no legal recourse for victims of harassment or abuse related to their LGBTQ+ status. This legal void contributes to the social invisibility and marginalization of the LGBTQ+ community.

The conservative cultural and religious norms are widespread across the country, and the government's enforcement policies apply broadly. Urban centers like Cairo and Alexandria may offer slightly more anonymity or underground support networks due to their size and diversity, but this does not translate into legal protection or greater social acceptance.

Overall, the country's legal and social environment remains uniformly unsupportive and discriminatory toward LGBTQ+ individuals.

## LGBTQ Tourism and Safety Concerns

LGBTQ tourism in Egypt is **extremely limited and undeveloped** due to the country's conservative social norms and restrictive legal environment. Unlike some other popular tourist destinations, Egypt does not have an established or openly welcoming scene for LGBTQ travelers. The prevailing cultural attitudes and government policies create an atmosphere where LGBTQ visitors must exercise considerable caution.

There are no particular areas in Egypt that are widely recognized as more tolerant or safer for LGBTQ individuals. While large cities such as Cairo and Alexandria are somewhat more cosmopolitan and diverse, this does not necessarily mean greater acceptance or safety for LGBTQ visitors. The country as a whole maintains conservative social values, and the lack of legal protections applies uniformly across regions. Underground or private gatherings may exist discreetly, but there are no public LGBTQ-friendly districts or venues comparable to those in more liberal countries.

Public displays of affection between LGBTQ visitors are generally not acceptable in Egypt and are strongly discouraged. Such behavior risks attracting negative attention from both local residents and law enforcement. Open expressions of romantic or sexual affection between same-sex couples can lead to harassment, discrimination, or even arrest under laws related to public morality. Visitors are advised to be discreet and respectful of local customs to avoid conflict.

**Safety concerns for LGBTQ visitors to Egypt are significant**. The risk of discrimination, harassment, or arrest exists, particularly if one is perceived to be violating social norms or local laws. Police may detain individuals suspected of homosexual conduct under ambiguous charges, and travelers could face invasive medical examinations or other abuses. Additionally, societal stigma means that LGBTQ visitors might encounter hostility or violence in public spaces. Given these risks, it is crucial for LGBTQ tourists to exercise caution, avoid public displays of affection, and stay informed about local laws and customs when traveling in Egypt.

 **General Questions**

1. ***Do laws in Egypt protect homosexual expressions and conduct?*** **No.** Laws in Egypt do not protect homosexual expressions or conduct. Instead, individuals suspected of engaging in same-sex relationships often face prosecution under broad laws related to public morality, debauchery, or prostitution. There are no legal safeguards or protections for LGBTQ+ expressions or conduct in the country.

2. ***What is the punishment for homosexual expressions and conduct?*** In Egypt, while same-sex relationships are not directly outlawed, people suspected of engaging in homosexual behavior are frequently prosecuted using laws against "debauchery," "public morality," or "prostitution." The penalties can include imprisonment for several months to several years, fines, and sometimes forced medical examinations. The severity of the punishment depends on the specific charges and situation, but those accused often endure harsh treatment from authorities.

## Law of the Land True Story[10]

The case of Andrew Medhat, an engineering student sentenced to three years in prison after arranging a date through a dating app, highlights the systemic targeting of LGBTQ people. Unbeknownst to him, the man he had been messaging was an undercover officer. After his arrest, police falsely told his family he was involved in sex work, further stigmatizing him and justifying the charges.

Since the late 1990s—and especially after the 2013 military coup—Egyptian authorities have intensified their crackdown on LGBTQ communities. Using dating apps like Grindr, police now routinely entrap people, fabricate evidence, and coerce confessions. The legal system offers little protection. Families, fearing public shame, often choose lawyers recommended by police, who rarely act in the accused's best interest. Medhat's lawyer advised him to plead guilty and then failed to appear in court. Meanwhile, those detained face abusive treatment, including beatings and invasive anal exams—practices widely condemned by human rights groups.

This repression is not only moralistic but political. Experts argue that the regime uses control over public morality and personal behavior to maintain order and reinforce its authority. LGBTQ people, already marginalized, are convenient targets. Yet amid this hostility, small signs of change are emerging. Younger Egyptians are showing more openness, and public support for personal privacy—particularly post-Arab Spring—has grown. Activists now focus on leveraging this concern for privacy to carve out space for rights without directly confronting social taboos.

---

10  https://www.theguardian.com/global-development-professionals-network/2017/apr/03/jailed-for-using-grindr-homosexuality-in-egypt

# SEXUALLY MOTIVATED/ VIOLENT CRIMES

# CHAPTER 9
# SEXUALLY MOTIVATED/ VIOLENT CRIMES

## Overview

Sexually motivated crimes are a widespread and ongoing issue in Egypt, particularly in the form of **sexual harassment, assault, and rape.** While comprehensive national crime statistics are difficult to obtain due to underreporting and lack of government transparency, multiple independent reports show the severity of the problem. A landmark **United Nations study in 2013** found that **99.3% of Egyptian women** surveyed had experienced some form of sexual harassment in their lifetime.[11] More recent data and reporting from human rights groups suggest that the issue remains deeply entrenched,  particularly in large cities such as Cairo and Alexandria.

Several social, cultural, and economic factors contribute to the high incidence of these crimes. Egypt's **patriarchal social structure**, which often normalizes male dominance and downplays women's autonomy, plays a key role. Cultural taboos around discussing sexuality and **widespread victim-blaming** discourage survivors from speaking out or seeking justice. A 2021 report from Human Rights Watch detailed how survivors of sexual violence often face hostility, humiliation, and legal risks

---

11  https://www.unwomen.org/en/news/stories/2013/4/
    press-release-on-study-of-harassment-against-women-in-egypt

when reporting crimes, particularly in high-profile or publicized cases. Additionally, high youth unemployment, economic instability, and overcrowding in urban areas have also been cited as contributing factors to the rise in harassment and assault.

Women and girls are overwhelmingly the primary victims, though men and boys have also reported abuse—particularly in **institutional settings** like detention centers. Vulnerable groups such as **refugees, migrants, domestic workers**, and low-income women face elevated risks due to limited access to protection, legal support, or public advocacy. A report by Amnesty International emphasized that refugees, especially women and LGBTQ+ individuals, are at particularly high risk of sexual abuse and exploitation.

There are regional disparities in how sexual crimes are reported and addressed. **Urban centers** such as Cairo and Giza often see higher reporting rates, though this may reflect greater public awareness and media attention rather than actual prevalence. In contrast, in **rural areas and Upper Egypt**, stricter social norms, gender segregation, and limited access to legal channels result in severe underreporting. In many rural communities, sexual offenses are often handled through **informal mediation or tribal reconciliation**, which frequently favors the perpetrator and silences the victim.

Despite growing awareness, systemic change remains slow. Some reforms have been introduced—such as the **2020 law guaranteeing anonymity for survivors of sexual assault**—but these have not substantially altered the underlying dynamics of impunity and stigma. Continued advocacy by women's rights organizations and legal aid groups offers hope for long-term change, but entrenched social attitudes and institutional shortcomings continue to pose serious obstacles.

## Related Legislation

In Egypt, the legal framework surrounding sexually motivated crimes includes several statutes meant to penalize sexual harassment, assault, and rape, but enforcement remains inconsistent and often insufficient, especially when cases involve gender-based violence.

The **Egyptian Penal Code** criminalizes rape and sexual assault under various articles. **Article 267** stipulates that a man who forces a woman to have sexual intercourse can face a **sentence of life imprisonment or death** if accompanied by aggravating circumstances (such as the use of a weapon or multiple perpetrators). **Article 268** covers sexual assault and stipulates **imprisonment for three to fifteen years**, depending on the severity and whether the victim is a minor or incapacitated.

Sexual harassment was not formally criminalized until 2014, when **Law No. 50 of 2014** amended the Penal Code to define and penalize harassment. Under this amendment, **verbal, physical, behavioral, phone, or online harassment** in public or private spaces is punishable by a **minimum of six months in prison and a fine of at least 3,000 EGP (about $60 USD)**, with harsher penalties if the perpetrator has authority over the victim or repeats the offense.

In 2020, Egypt passed a law guaranteeing the **anonymity of survivors** of sexual violence, aiming to protect victims from social stigma and legal retaliation when filing complaints. This was a response to public outcry over several high-profile cases, including the "Fairmont crime" involving gang rape of a woman at a luxury hotel in 2014 (see Law of the Land True Story below).

However, enforcement of these laws remains highly problematic. Police and judicial authorities are **often reluctant to pursue cases**, and many victims report being dismissed, blamed, or even harassed themselves when seeking help. Investigations are slow, forensic procedures are outdated, and there is a general **lack of victim-sensitive practices** in law enforcement and courts. In many rural or conservative areas, victims are pressured to settle matters privately, sometimes even being forced to marry their attacker.

Furthermore, **same-sex sexual assault victims** or individuals perceived as LGBTQ+ are often denied justice entirely or even face arrest themselves under "public morality" laws, adding another layer of legal vulnerability for marginalized communities.

## General Questions

1. *Do laws in Egypt related to sex crimes protect the victims equally?* **No.** Laws in Egypt related to sex crimes **do not protect all victims equally**. While the Egyptian Penal Code includes provisions criminalizing rape, sexual assault, and harassment, their enforcement is inconsistent and often biased, particularly against women, LGBTQ+ individuals, and marginalized groups. Victims frequently face social stigma, police mistreatment, and legal hurdles when reporting crimes. In some cases, especially involving **male or LGBTQ+ survivors**, victims themselves risk prosecution under vague morality laws. Cultural norms and institutional discrimination further prevent equal protection under the law, making justice inaccessible for many.

2. *Pursuant to law, what is the age of consent in Egypt?* Under Egyptian law, the age of consent for sexual activity is **18**. Any sexual act involving a person under this age is considered **illegal**, regardless of whether the minor consents. The Penal Code treats such acts as statutory rape or indecent assault, and they carry mandatory prison sentences. Courts do not recognize consent from anyone under 18, and there are no legal exceptions for close-in-age relationships.

## Law of the Land True Story[12]

The Fairmont trial is one of Egypt's most infamous recent cases involving sexual violence and the suppression of survivors. In 2014, a young woman was drugged and gang-raped by a group of men during a private party at the Fairmont Nile City Hotel in Cairo. The incident

---

12  https://www.bbc.com/news/world-middle-east-57072192

was recorded on video and circulated among wealthy social circles. The case remained buried for years until 2020, when survivors and activists brought it to light on social media, triggering public outrage and renewed calls for justice.

Instead of swiftly prosecuting the accused, Egyptian authorities arrested several witnesses and activists who had helped expose the crime. Some were detained, interrogated, and even subjected to forced virginity tests. Meanwhile, many of the accused fled the country. Although Interpol issued red notices and some suspects were later extradited, the Egyptian prosecution eventually dropped the case in 2022, citing insufficient evidence.

The Fairmont case highlighted not only the brutality of sexual violence in elite circles but also how the justice system can be used to silence survivors and protect the powerful. Despite national and international attention, the trial ended without justice for the victim, reflecting the broader challenges faced by survivors of sexual assault in Egypt.

 ## Takeaways

- Despite laws criminalizing rape, assault, and harassment, sexual violence remains pervasive across Egypt.

- The Penal Code outlines strict penalties for rape and harassment, yet survivors often face police negligence, victim-blaming, or legal jeopardy themselves. LGBTQ+ individuals and male survivors are particularly vulnerable to arrest under vague morality laws.

- Authorities have used dating apps to entrap individuals—especially gay men—and prosecute them under charges like "public debauchery." In some cases, victims are also subjected to torture or forced anal exams in detention.

- Survivors often lack access to supportive legal counsel, as families may defer to lawyers aligned with police. Social shame and fear of exposure drive many to stay silent, especially in conservative or rural areas.

- The Fairmont Hotel gang rape case revealed how justice can be obstructed even with strong public attention. Witnesses were jailed, suspects fled, and the trial was ultimately dropped—underscoring the deep institutional resistance to holding perpetrators accountable.

CHAPTER 10

# ARRESTED IN EGYPT

## IN THIS CHAPTER

- Overview
- Arrest Process
- Getting Legal Assistance
- Bail
- Complaints Against Police
- General Questions

# ARRESTED IN EGYPT

## Overview

When traveling in a foreign country, it's imperative to recognize that you are subject to the legal jurisdiction and regulations of that nation. These laws may significantly differ from those in your home country and might not offer the same legal protections you are accustomed to. It's crucial to bear in mind that penalties for violating foreign laws can be more severe than those for similar offenses in your home country, and ignorance of these laws is not typically accepted as a defense.

The consequences for breaking the law while abroad can be severe and may include expulsion, fines, arrest, or imprisonment. Even unintentional violations can lead to serious legal repercussions. It is essential for travelers to be aware of and adhere to the laws of the host country to avoid legal entanglements and ensure a safe and enjoyable experience.

Specifically, stringent penalties are often enforced for possession, use, or trafficking of illegal drugs in many countries. Convicted offenders can expect severe consequences, including lengthy jail sentences and hefty fines. The legal processes for foreigners in the event of an arrest abroad involve being charged or indicted, prosecuted, potentially convicted and sentenced, and, if applicable, going through an appeals process.

Navigating a foreign legal system can be complex, and individuals arrested abroad must be prepared to comply with the legal procedures of the host country. Seeking legal representation and understanding the local legal nuances are crucial steps for those facing legal issues in a foreign jurisdiction.

Awareness of and adherence to the laws of a foreign country are paramount when traveling. Understanding the potential consequences for legal violations and being prepared to navigate the legal system of the host country are essential aspects of responsible international travel.

## Arrest Process

In Egypt, the arrest process is governed by the **Egyptian Code of Criminal Procedure**. Individuals can be arrested either with a warrant issued by the Public Prosecution or, in certain situations, without one—such as when a person is caught in the act of committing a crime ("flagrante delicto").

Once arrested, the individual is typically taken to a local police station, where they may be detained and questioned. By law, authorities must present the detainee to the Public Prosecutor **within 48 hours**. The prosecutor then decides whether to release the person or authorize **pre-trial detention**, which can last for an initial period of up to **15 days**. This period may be renewed repeatedly—often in 15- to 45-day increments—based on the nature of the crime, with no formal limit in some national security cases.

While the law guarantees the **right to legal counsel**, in practice, access to a lawyer during arrest and initial interrogation is not always upheld. Suspects may be questioned without their attorney present, and some report being denied contact with family or legal representatives for extended periods.

Egyptian law also prohibits torture and inhumane treatment, but international human rights groups have **documented cases of physical abuse, prolonged solitary confinement, and forced confessions**. Complaints of mistreatment often go uninvestigated. Foreign nationals arrested in Egypt follow the same judicial process but may face additional complications. These include **language barriers, restrictions on communication with embassies**, and the potential for **longer detentions** due to bureaucratic delays.

Once formal charges are filed, the case moves toward **investigation or trial**, depending on the severity and type of offense. Defendants may remain in detention during this phase, especially if the court deems them a flight risk or a threat to public order.

## Getting Legal Assistance

In Egypt, the law guarantees every individual the **right to legal representation**, whether they are an Egyptian citizen or a foreign national. Article 124 of the Egyptian Criminal Procedure Code prohibits the prosecution from interrogating a suspect in a felony case without first notifying their lawyer. If the suspect does not have one, the law requires the appointment of a defense attorney. However, this legal right is **not always respected in practice**. Particularly during the early hours of detention, detainees may be questioned without legal counsel, and delays in accessing a lawyer are common.

Foreign nationals are entitled to the same legal protections as Egyptians, with the added right—under the Vienna Convention on Consular Relations—to contact their embassy or consulate. After arrest, they should be allowed to notify their diplomatic mission, which can assist in finding a lawyer, informing family members, and providing an interpreter. Despite this obligation, Egyptian authorities do not always grant timely consular access, especially in politically sensitive or high-profile cases.

While the law permits access to free legal representation in serious criminal cases, the system has serious limitations. Court-appointed lawyers, available to those who cannot afford private counsel, are often overworked, underpaid, and unable to dedicate sufficient time to their cases. This problem is even more acute for foreign nationals, who may also face language barriers, cultural misunderstandings, and a lack of familiarity with Egypt's legal environment. Unlike in countries with a public defender system, Egypt does not have a dedicated corps of full-time, state-supported attorneys providing consistent legal aid to indigent defendants.

Although a few non-governmental organizations offer legal assistance to vulnerable populations—such as migrants, refugees, and political detainees—resources are limited. Groups like the **Egyptian Initiative for Personal Rights and the Refugee Legal Aid Project** at the American University in Cairo provide some support, but demand often outstrips capacity. As a result, most foreign nationals are best served by turning to their consulate for help in securing reputable private legal counsel.

If a foreign visitor is arrested in Egypt, it is crucial to request immediate contact with both legal counsel and their consulate. It is advisable not to sign any documents unless fully understood, especially without translation. Remaining calm and cooperative during police interactions may help ease the situation, and recording or remembering the names of officers or arrest details can prove useful later in one's defense. While embassies cannot interfere directly in legal proceedings or secure a detainee's release, they can monitor treatment, ensure basic rights are observed, and assist in locating reliable attorneys.

## Bail

Egypt does have a form of bail system, but it operates differently from systems found in countries like the United States. Bail in Egypt is **not guaranteed**, and whether it is granted depends largely on the discretion of the public prosecutor or the judge overseeing the case. After arrest and initial questioning, the prosecution may choose to release the accused pending further investigation, either without conditions or on the condition that bail is paid. Bail amounts can vary significantly depending on the seriousness of the charge, the perceived flight risk, and the individual's financial circumstances. In many cases, particularly for minor offenses, release may be granted without monetary bail but with restrictions such as travel bans or regular check-ins with the police.

For foreigners, bail decisions are often more complicated. Egyptian authorities may view non-citizens as a higher flight risk, making them less likely to be released. If bail is granted, the court may impose strict conditions, including surrendering passports or staying within the country for the duration of the investigation. In some cases, travel bans remain in place even after bail is posted, and visitors may be barred from leaving the country for weeks or months.

The amount set for bail is often arbitrary and can be prohibitively high, especially for serious offenses. There is no standard schedule or system for calculating bail based on income or crime category. Additionally, in politically sensitive or national security cases, pretrial detention is often preferred over bail, and individuals may remain in custody for extended periods without a conviction.

## Complaints Against Police

The reputation of Egypt's police force is **deeply polarized**. While some Egyptians view the police as a necessary force for maintaining order, especially in crowded urban centers, others see them as instruments of state repression. Over the past decade, Egypt's security services—especially the Ministry of Interior and its various branches—have been frequently accused of **corruption, abuse of power, and human rights violations**.

The most common complaints against the police include arbitrary arrests, excessive use of force, verbal and physical abuse, prolonged pretrial detention, and in more serious cases, torture and enforced disappearances. Allegations often arise from encounters during protests, in detention centers, or in police stations. Human rights groups have also documented mistreatment of marginalized communities, including political activists, LGBTQ+ individuals, refugees, and low-income residents.

Filing a complaint against the police in Egypt can be challenging and, in some cases, risky—especially if the complaint involves state security or politically sensitive issues. Officially, complaints can be submitted to the

**Public Prosecution**, the **Ministry of Interior**, or the **National Council for Human Rights (NCHR)**. However, follow-through is inconsistent, and complainants often face delays, indifference, or even retaliation.

For those seeking independent channels, several human rights organizations have documented abuses and, in some cases, offered legal support. While many domestic organizations have been forced to close or restrict their operations in recent years, a few continue to work, often with limited capacity. Notable groups include:

### Egyptian Initiative for Personal Rights (EIPR)

**Website:** https://eipr.org/en
**Email:** eipr@eipr.org

### Cairo Institute for Human Rights Studies (CIHRS)

**Website:** https://cihrs.org
**Email:** info@cihrs.org

### Refugee Legal Aid Project (RLAP), American University in Cairo

**Website:** https://schools.aucegypt.edu/research/src/rll.aspx

It's important to note that operating space for human rights defenders in Egypt remains extremely restricted. Foreign nationals who experience misconduct by the police should always notify their embassy or consulate immediately, as this is often the safest and most effective path to raise concerns and seek support.

# General Questions

1. *If I am convicted in Egypt, am I likely to be released on bail pending the outcome of my appeal?* If you are convicted in Egypt, you are generally not released on bail while your appeal is pending. Once a sentence is issued—especially in felony cases—it is typically enforced immediately, even if an appeal is filed. Release pending appeal is rare and usually limited to minor offenses. Foreign nationals face the same restrictions, and in politically sensitive cases, the chance of post-conviction release is extremely low. In most cases, you should expect to remain in custody during the appeal process, which can take months or even longer.

2. *What influences a bail determination?* Bail in Egypt is decided by prosecutors or judges and depends on factors like the **seriousness of the crime**, **flight risk**, **criminal history**, and potential to **interfere with the investigation**. Foreign nationals are often seen as high flight risks, making bail less likely. In sensitive cases, bail is rarely granted, and amounts can vary widely with no fixed standards.

3. *Who is entitled to bail?* In Egypt, **bail is not a guaranteed right** but may be granted at the discretion of the prosecutor or judge. It is more commonly allowed in misdemeanor cases or minor offenses.

   For felonies, **especially** serious or political crimes, bail is rarely granted. Anyone accused of a crime may be considered for bail, but approval depends on the case details—not on entitlement by law.

4. *If I am arrested, how soon will I see a judge or magistrate?* If you are arrested in Egypt, the law requires that you be brought before the Public Prosecutor **within 48 hours**. The prosecutor, not a judge, makes the initial decision on detention, release, or bail. You may not appear before a judge until much later—often days or even weeks—especially if the prosecutor authorizes ongoing pretrial detention. Judicial review typically happens only after multiple renewals or if the case proceeds to trial.

5. *Will I be able to contact my country's embassy in Egypt?* **Yes.** If you are arrested in Egypt, you have the right to contact your country's embassy or consulate under the **Vienna Convention on Consular Relations**. Egyptian authorities are required to inform you of this right and allow communication. However, in practice, access may be delayed, especially in politically sensitive or national security cases. It's important to insist on consular contact early, as your embassy can help arrange legal representation, notify your family, and monitor your treatment.

# JAILS VS. PRISONS: CONDITIONS & CULTURE

# JAILS VS. PRISONS: CONDITIONS & CULTURE

## Overview

In Egypt's criminal justice system, jails and prisons serve different functions, although the terms are sometimes used interchangeably in conversation. **Jails** are primarily used for holding individuals who are **awaiting trial**, **under investigation**, or **serving very short sentences**—typically less than three months. These facilities are often referred to locally as *habs* or *habs ihtiyāti* (pretrial detention). **Prisons**, on the other hand, are meant for individuals who have been **convicted of crimes** and are **serving longer sentences**. They house those found guilty of more serious offenses, including felonies and national security crimes.

Both jails and prisons fall **under the control of the Ministry of Interior** and are operated through the **General Directorate of Prisons**. While the administrative structure is national, local police departments are often responsible for short-term detention centers. The most critical challenge is **overcrowding.** Human rights organizations such as Human Rights Watch and the Egyptian Commission for Rights and Freedoms have noted that many prisons and jails operate far above capacity, leading to poor living conditions. Legal access in pretrial detention is often limited, and detainees sometimes face long delays before being brought to court. Although Egyptian law caps pretrial detention at two years, it is common for individuals to remain in custody far beyond that limit, turning jails into de facto long-term holding centers.

Likewise, **conditions** in both jails and prisons are a **major concern.**
Reports have documented serious deficiencies in medical care, hygiene,
and access to basic necessities. Facilities like Tora Prison and Badr
Prison, which house high-profile or political prisoners, have been the
subject of international criticism for allegations of abuse and neglect.
Egypt is also known to use its detention system to hold political oppo-
nents, journalists, and activists under vague charges such as "spreading
false news" or "belonging to a banned group." These individuals may be
detained in high-security prisons or even in undisclosed locations that
function as secret prisons operated by intelligence agencies.

Another distinctive feature of Egypt's system is the use of military courts
and detention for civilians accused of certain crimes, particularly terrorism or actions deemed to threaten national security. Detainees in these
cases may be held in **military prisons**, where oversight is limited and
conditions are often more secretive. Additionally, facilities for women,
such as Qanater Women's Prison, and juvenile detention centers exist,
but enforcement of gender- and age-specific protections is inconsistent.
Despite legal frameworks, discrimination and mistreatment persist, especially for vulnerable groups.

In sum, while jails and prisons in Egypt are formally distinct in purpose—short-term vs. long-term detention—the country's practice often
blurs that line. Due process issues, extended pretrial detention, poor
conditions, and political use of incarceration are key characteristics of
how Egypt's detention system operates today.

## Prison Conditions and Living Environment

Prison conditions in Egypt are marked by **overcrowding, limited access to basic services, and concerns over human rights abuses.**
Housing arrangements in prisons are generally based on security levels
and inmate classification, though in practice this system is inconsistent.
Facilities like **Badr** and **Scorpion** prisons are known for their **high-security wings**, which often house political detainees, journalists, and individuals accused of terrorism-related offenses. Inmates in these facilities are frequently subjected to solitary confinement, minimal exercise

time, and restricted visitation rights. While **lower-security prisons** exist for individuals serving sentences for non-violent crimes, overcrowding often leads to mixed classifications, with pretrial detainees and convicted criminals sharing cells, despite legal requirements for separation.

**Access to health care** in Egyptian prisons remains one of the most criticized aspects of the detention system. Although Egyptian law mandates the provision of medical care, in practice, access is often delayed, insufficient, or entirely denied. Prisons are generally understaffed with medical professionals, and clinics within facilities frequently lack necessary medications and equipment. Detainees with chronic illnesses or serious health conditions may experience long waiting times for outside hospital referrals or receive no specialized care at all. Reports from organizations like Amnesty International and Human Rights Watch have highlighted cases where the denial of treatment has led to preventable deaths in custody. Requests for independent medical examinations or humanitarian release on health grounds are rarely granted, especially for political prisoners.

**Food quality and sanitation** inside Egyptian prisons are also major issues. Inmates often rely on food brought by family members during visits, as the meals provided by the prison system are frequently described as nutritionally inadequate and unhygienic. Access to clean drinking water, soap, and toilet facilities is limited in many prisons, and personal hygiene items are not regularly supplied. Cells are often overcrowded and poorly ventilated, with insufficient bedding and exposure to extreme heat or cold depending on the season. In some facilities, prisoners report infestations of insects or vermin. Those without family support are especially vulnerable to deprivation, as they cannot supplement the poor conditions through care packages or bribes.

Overall, the living environment in Egyptian prisons **fails to meet international standards**. Despite government claims of prison reform, independent investigations and testimonies from former detainees point to a system plagued by neglect, punitive treatment, and systemic human rights violations.

## Inmate Rights and Legal Protections

In Egypt, inmates are formally granted a set of constitutional and legal rights, but the reality inside prisons often falls far short of these protections. According to **Article 55 of Egypt's 2014 Constitution**, "All those who are arrested, detained or have their freedom restricted shall be treated in a manner that preserves their dignity." The law prohibits torture, inhumane treatment, and arbitrary detention. It also guarantees the right to due process, access to legal representation, and communication with family. However, these rights are frequently undermined by widespread violations, particularly in cases involving political detainees or individuals charged under Egypt's broad national security laws.

In theory, prisoners are **entitled to access legal counsel and to file appeals or complaints** with the courts. Detainees have the right to meet privately with their lawyers, challenge the legality of their detention, and appeal both pretrial detention orders and final convictions. In practice, these rights are **often delayed or denied**. Many detainees, particularly in high-security prisons, report being held incommunicado for extended periods, denied timely access to attorneys, or transferred to courtrooms without prior legal consultation. Legal resources such as prison law libraries are virtually nonexistent, and inmates depend almost entirely on outside counsel and family for legal assistance.

Reports from human rights organizations consistently document patterns of abuse inside Egyptian prisons. These include **physical violence, sexual abuse, prolonged solitary confinement, psychological intimidation, and the denial of medical care as a punitive measure.** Torture and mistreatment have been reported during both interrogation and incarceration, especially in facilities operated by the National Security Agency. Although torture is banned under both Egyptian law and international conventions to which Egypt is a signatory, complaints rarely result in prosecution or meaningful accountability. In theory, inmates have **the right to file complaints through the Public Prosecutor's Office or the National Council for Human Rights**, but such mechanisms are limited in independence and rarely produce action. In some cases, those who attempt to report abuse face retaliation from prison authorities.

## ? General Questions

1. *What is the difference between a jail and prison in Egypt?*
   In Egypt, the main difference between a jail and a prison lies in
   purpose and duration. **Jails** (*habs ihtiyāti*) are used for **pretrial
   detention** or **short sentences**, typically less than three months.
   They often hold people awaiting investigation, trial, or appeal.
   **Prisons** (*sijn*) are for those **convicted and serving longer sentences**, especially for serious crimes. Jails are usually attached to
   police stations and run locally, while prisons fall under national
   oversight by the Ministry of Interior. Due to overcrowding and
   delays, people often remain in jails for extended periods, blurring
   the line between the two.

2. *Do jails and prisons offer religious services to inmates?*
   **Yes**. Jails and prisons in Egypt do offer religious services, mainly
   for Muslims and Christians. Most facilities have spaces for prayer,
   and the Ministry of Interior organizes Islamic events and allows
   religious leaders to visit. Christian inmates, especially Copts, can
   attend chapel services, and some prisons like Wadi al-Natroun
   have built churches inside. However, **access may vary depending
   on the facility, security level, or inmate's religion**, and there
   have been reports of some inmates being denied access to services despite formal policies allowing them.

3. *How do prisoners spend their time?* Prisoners in Egypt spend
   their time under strict routines, but the quality of daily life varies
   by facility and security level. Inmates typically spend long hours
   confined to overcrowded cells with limited movement. Some
   prisons allow short periods for exercise or fresh air, but these
   are not guaranteed and may be denied, especially in high-security wings. Access to books, television, or radio depends on the
   prison's resources and the inmate's privileges. Religious practices and prayer are common daily activities, particularly among
   Muslim inmates. Inmates with outside support may receive food
   or supplies from family, which can significantly improve their
   daily conditions. Overall, daily life is heavily restricted, and many

prisoners experience long stretches of inactivity, isolation, and limited access to programs or education.

4. *What type of jobs can inmates perform?* In Egyptian prisons, inmates may be assigned to various types of labor, depending on the facility, security level, and the nature of their offense. Common jobs include kitchen work, cleaning, laundry, maintenance, and agricultural labor in prison farms. Some prisons also have workshops where inmates produce furniture, textiles, or crafts as part of state-run vocational programs. These jobs are generally low-paid or unpaid, and participation is often not optional. While authorities promote such work as rehabilitation, critics argue that it can amount to forced labor, especially when inmates are denied wages or work under harsh conditions.

5. *How does the prison commissary system work in Egypt?* In Egyptian prisons, the commissary system allows inmates to buy extra food and supplies beyond the basic prison provisions. Families usually deposit money into inmates' accounts so they can purchase items like snacks or hygiene products. However, prices in prison canteens are often much higher than outside, and access is sometimes limited—especially in high-security prisons where family visits and deliveries may be restricted. There are also reports of corruption, with guards demanding bribes to allow visits or pass on goods. Overall, while the commissary helps supplement inmates' needs, problems like inflated prices, restricted access, and exploitation are common.

6. *What type of medical care do prisoners receive?* Prisoners in Egypt often face poor access to medical care. While the law requires health services, many prisons have limited medical staff and supplies. Inmates frequently rely on family to bring medicines, but these can be confiscated, especially in high-security prisons like Scorpion. Chronic and serious illnesses often go untreated or face delays, sometimes leading to severe health deterioration or death. Overcrowding and poor sanitation worsen health conditions. Overall, medical care in Egyptian prisons is inadequate and falls short of legal and international standards.

7. ***What is prison culture like in Egypt?*** Prison culture in Egypt is shaped by **overcrowding**, **strict control**, and a **harsh environment**. Inmates often face tough conditions marked by limited personal space, constant surveillance, and strict rules enforced by guards. Hierarchies among prisoners can develop based on factors like length of sentence, connections, or gang affiliations, influencing daily life and access to resources. Religious practices play an important role in coping, with many inmates turning to faith for comfort and community. However, violence, intimidation, and corruption are common, with guards sometimes abusing their power and inmates facing exploitation or mistreatment. Overall, Egyptian prison culture is one of survival amid challenging and often oppressive conditions.

# HELPING A FRIEND OR RELATIVE IMPRISONED IN EGYPT

# HELPING A FRIEND OR RELATIVE IMPRISONED IN EGYPT

## Overview

If a family member or friend is imprisoned in Egypt while abroad, there are important steps to take to protect their rights and provide support. First, **immediately notify your country's embassy or consulate in Egypt**. The embassy can offer assistance such as providing a list of English-speaking attorneys, helping ensure fair treatment, monitoring the detainee's condition, and facilitating communication with family. They can also help connect you with local lawyers, offer guidance on navigating the legal system, and visit the detainee to check on their wellbeing.

It's important to **obtain reliable legal representation as soon as possible**. Hiring a skilled lawyer familiar with Egypt's judicial system is crucial since delays, limited access to evidence, and lengthy pretrial detention are common. Other practical advice includes maintaining regular communication with the detainee if possible, sending care packages if allowed, and documenting all interactions with authorities. Understand that Egypt's legal process can be slow and opaque, so patience and persistence are key.

## Sending Food, Supplies, and Money to an Inmate

In Egypt, families and friends can bring food and supplies to inmates, but there are strict rules and varying practices depending on the prison. In most facilities, food deliveries are allowed during designated visitation days. Home-cooked meals, dry goods, bottled water, and packaged snacks are typically permitted, but **all items are subject to inspection.** Foods with liquids (like soups or sauces), sharp utensils, and anything perishable or considered a security risk may be rejected. In high-security prisons like Scorpion or Badr, authorities have been known to arbitrarily restrict or block food deliveries altogether.

Packages may also be allowed but are tightly regulated. Commonly **allowed items** include **clothes, soap, toothpaste,** and **over-the-counter medications. Prohibited items** include **electronics, books with political or religious content,** and **anything deemed a threat to security**. Guards inspect all items, and some may be confiscated without explanation. In certain cases, prisoners are denied access to delivered packages entirely, especially if they are held under national security or terrorism charges.

**Sending money** to inmates is **possible through prison accounts**. Families can deposit funds during visits, which the inmate can then use to purchase items from the prison commissary. The process is handled in person, usually at the prison's administrative office, and may require the inmate's ID number and confirmation from prison staff. However, there are frequent complaints of delays, unexplained account freezes, or demands for bribes to process transactions or allow purchases.

Due to inconsistent enforcement and corruption, it's essential for families to confirm procedures directly with prison staff and to bring official ID when visiting or delivering items. Keeping receipts and a record of all attempts to deliver food or money is also advised in case of disputes or denials.

## Mail, Phone Calls, and Visitation

In theory, inmates in Egypt are allowed to receive mail, but **in practice**, the **process is inconsistent and often restricted**. Letters may be **censored, delayed**, or **blocked entirely**, especially for prisoners held on political or national security charges. Many families report that mail never reaches the inmate or is intercepted without explanation. Incoming and outgoing correspondence is subject to inspection by prison authorities.

Inmates are not allowed to possess cell phones under any circumstances. Phone calls are allowed in some prisons, but there is no uniform policy across all facilities. Where permitted, **calls must be made through monitored landlines** during limited hours and with prior authorization. Access is more likely in lower-security prisons or for inmates with good behavior records. High-security and pretrial detention facilities often restrict phone use altogether.

**Visits are generally allowed**, though the frequency and conditions **vary by facility and the nature of the charges**. Close family members—such as spouses, parents, and children—are typically permitted to visit. Friends may be allowed with prior approval. Visits usually occur once every 15–30 days and must be scheduled in advance. All visitors must present a valid ID and may be subject to security checks. Physical contact is often restricted, and conversations are usually monitored. In high-security prisons, visits can be conducted behind glass or even denied altogether without clear justification.

## Prison Scams

Scams related to prisoners in Egypt are a known issue, often targeting the families of detainees—especially foreigners unfamiliar with the legal system. These scams typically involve individuals who falsely claim they can secure early release, improve prison conditions, or arrange access to restricted services like phones or visits, usually in exchange for money. In some cases, people impersonate lawyers or government officials and promise guaranteed outcomes for large sums. Others include corrupt prison staff demanding unofficial payments to deliver food, allow visitations, or process commissary deposits.

Red flags include **urgent requests for cash without receipts, vague promises of influence or inside connections,** and **pressure to keep the transaction secret or avoid contacting the embassy.** If someone refuses to provide proper identification or documentation, that is also a sign of potential fraud.

If you think you're being scammed, stop communication immediately and avoid making any payments. Contact your embassy for help verifying identities and navigating prison procedures. Embassies can offer guidance, recommend legitimate lawyers, and help protect your rights and those of the detainee. Staying cautious and working through formal, documented channels is essential to avoiding exploitation in Egypt's often secretive prison system. If you've already made a payment and suspect fraud, report it to both your embassy and local Egyptian authorities, although the chances of recovery or legal action may be limited. Keep a written record of all interactions and share any evidence you have. Reaching out to reputable human rights organizations or legal aid groups in Egypt may also help, especially in politically sensitive cases or situations involving abuse or bribery.

## Upon Release

Foreigners released from prison or jail in Egypt are often subject to additional rules and restrictions beyond their sentence. In many cases, they are issued **a deportation order** and must leave the country within a set time frame, often immediately upon release. If they are not deported right away, they may be required to report to immigration authorities or remain in Egypt until court proceedings—such as an appeal—are finalized. Some individuals are placed on **travel ban lists,** preventing them from leaving the country without special permission.

Additional legal obligations can include **mandatory court check-ins, restrictions on movement,** or **being barred from re-entering Egypt for a certain period,** especially if the conviction involved national security, drugs, or political offenses. In some cases, authorities confiscate passports during the legal process and return them only once the case is fully closed.

Foreigners should contact their embassy immediately upon release for help navigating exit procedures and ensuring compliance with Egyptian immigration and legal requirements. A local attorney may also be needed to confirm whether any court-imposed conditions still apply.

# THE ADMINISTRATION OF JUSTICE

# THE ADMINISTRATION OF JUSTICE

## Egypt's Legal System[13]

The Egyptian legal system has deep historical roots that span several civilizations, evolving through **Pharaonic, Islamic,** and **colonial influences** into its current hybrid form. Historically, ancient Egypt had a centralized legal authority where the pharaoh acted as supreme judge, and laws were often unwritten but grounded in principles of **Ma'at**—truth, justice, and order. During the Islamic era, **Sharia law** became dominant, administered through religious judges known as **qadis.** Under **Ottoman rule** (1517–1805), Islamic legal traditions were maintained, though local customs continued to shape enforcement. Egypt's **modern legal system** began taking shape in the 19th century under Muhammad Ali and his successors, who introduced sweeping legal reforms to modernize the state. Inspired by European, particularly French, models, these reforms included the **codification of laws** and the creation of **secular courts.** By the early 20th century, Egypt had adopted **civil codes** heavily influenced by the **Napoleonic Code,** especially in commercial and civil matters, while retaining **Sharia jurisdiction** over personal status issues.

The **key components** of the Egyptian legal system today include **civil law** (covering contracts, torts, property, and obligations), **criminal**

---

13   https://www.nyulawglobal.org/globalex/egypt1.html

law (governed by the Penal Code and Criminal Procedure Code), **administrative law** (covering state-related disputes), and **personal status law** (primarily based on religious principles). Egyptian law is **codified**, meaning that **statutes** are the primary source of law, and **judicial precedent** plays a limited role. The **Constitution** serves as the supreme legal authority, and **Article 2** declares that the **principles of Islamic Sharia** are the main source of legislation, making religion a cornerstone of certain legal domains.

Egypt's **judiciary** is structured in multiple layers, with different courts assigned specific roles. **Civil and criminal cases** begin in **Courts of First Instance**, which handle trials and initial rulings. Appeals from these courts go to the **Courts of Appeal**, which review both legal and factual elements of cases. The highest authority in the regular court system is the **Court of Cassation**, which focuses on **legal interpretation** and ensures consistency in applying the law across lower courts. **Administrative disputes**—those involving government actions, licenses, contracts, or civil service matters—fall under the jurisdiction of the **State Council** (*Majlis al-Dawla*), which operates independently from the civil judiciary. The **Supreme Constitutional Court** stands apart from all other courts and rules on the **constitutionality of laws**, resolves jurisdictional conflicts among courts, and interprets legislative provisions when necessary.

A **distinctive feature** of the Egyptian judiciary is the **parallel nature** of its court systems: the regular judiciary for civil and criminal matters, the State Council for administrative cases, and **exceptional courts** such as **military** and **emergency courts** that may handle cases involving civilians, especially during times of political unrest or under emergency law. **Military courts** can try civilians for crimes related to national security or offenses occurring in designated military zones. **Emergency courts**, which may be activated during a state of emergency, often handle politically sensitive cases with **limited appeal rights**. Egypt also maintains **religious-based courts** for personal status issues, primarily using **Islamic law for Muslims** and some **ecclesiastical rules for Christians**, though all fall under the oversight of the **state**.

**Challenges** to the judiciary in Egypt include concerns about **independence, political interference**, and **lack of transparency** in high-profile trials. Although the Constitution guarantees **judicial independence**, in practice, **appointments** and **promotions** of judges are often influenced by **executive preferences**. The **President appoints** top judges, and in politically sensitive cases—such as those involving activists, journalists, or opposition figures—courts have been accused of delivering verdicts that align with government interests. The use of **military and emergency courts** to try civilians has drawn international criticism for bypassing standard **due process** protections. Additionally, **procedural delays**, **case backlogs**, and **under-resourced courts** make it difficult for ordinary citizens to access timely justice. Legal reforms in **commercial law** and **digital services** are ongoing, but broader judicial reform—particularly in enhancing **transparency**, limiting **executive influence**, and ensuring **fair trial guarantees**—remains a significant challenge.

 ## General Questions

1. *Will the court treat first-time offenders and tourists with more leniency?* **No.** Egyptian courts **do not guarantee leniency** for first-time offenders or tourists. While judges may use discretion and sometimes issue lighter sentences for minor offenses or clean records, this depends on the case, the judge, and the circumstances. In general, **tourists are held to the same legal standards** as locals, and claiming ignorance of the law is not a defense.

2. *If I am charged with a crime, which court is likely to hear my case?* If you are charged with a crime in Egypt, your case will usually be heard by a **Court of First Instance**, which handles most criminal trials. For more serious crimes, it may go to a higher criminal court within the **Court of Appeal**. In exceptional cases—such as those involving national security or occurring in military zones—you could be tried in a military or emergency court, which offers fewer legal protections. The type of court depends on the severity and nature of the offense.

3. ***What is the standard of proof in a criminal case in Egypt?*** In Egypt, the standard of proof in a criminal case is that the judge must be convinced of the defendant's guilt **beyond a reasonable doubt**. However, this is not defined in strict legal terms as in some other systems. Judges have broad discretion to evaluate evidence, including confessions, witness testimony, and police reports, and they are not bound by strict rules of admissibility. There is no jury system, so the judge alone decides whether the prosecution has met the burden of proof.

 **Law of the Land True Story**[14]

Five young fishermen in their 20s were arrested in January, 2025 by military police from the Egypt Future Sustainable Development Agency (EFSDA). They were charged under the 2021 Lakes and Fisheries Protection law for fishing during a "prohibited period" and entering a "military area"—a section of Lake Bardawil near North Sinai designated as such in 2019 by presidential decree.

Lake Bardawil has traditionally been a vital source of livelihood for about 3,500 fishermen. However, from 2019, the lake was placed under military control—even though this territory had previously been administered by the civilian Lake Protection and Fish Wealth Development Authority.

The trial unfolded in a military court, not a civilian one, which human rights groups say violates international legal norms. Observers flagged serious violations: lawyers were not allowed to cross-examine prosecution witnesses, some hearings occurred without the defendants present, and the trial was based on decrees that were never published in the official gazette. The fishermen remain detained in a Central

---

14  https://www.theguardian.com/world/2025/may/28/
    egypt-illegally-detaining-alaa-abd-el-fattah-un-investigators-find

Security Forces camp in Ismailia—an unofficial detention site—raising concerns about arbitrary detention.

Human rights organizations, including Amnesty International and the Sinai Foundation for Human Rights, criticized the proceedings as a "travesty" and a "flagrant violation" of due process rights. They argue these trials exemplify a troubling trend: under recent laws and decrees, Egypt's military courts are able to try civilians for offenses that fall outside military jurisdiction, thereby undermining civilian judicial independence.

 **Takeaways**

- Egypt's legal system is a **hybrid of civil and Islamic law**, shaped by Pharaonic traditions, Sharia, Ottoman practices, and French legal influence introduced in the 19th century.

- The judiciary is **structured in tiers**, with Courts of First Instance handling most trials, Courts of Appeal reviewing decisions, and the Court of Cassation ensuring legal consistency. The Supreme Constitutional Court rules on constitutionality, and the State Council handles administrative disputes.

- Parallel and exceptional courts exist, including **military** and **emergency courts** that may try civilians, often with limited appeal rights. Religious courts manage personal status matters but remain under state authority.

- Judicial independence is **limited in practice**, with executive influence over appointments and verdicts in sensitive cases. Delays, backlogs, and resource constraints also affect the system's efficiency and fairness.

- Tourists and first-time offenders are **not guaranteed leniency**. All defendants face the same legal standards. Judges decide cases without juries and must be convinced beyond reasonable doubt, though they have broad discretion in weighing evidence.

CHAPTER 14

# CRIME VICTIM ASSISTANCE

# CRIME VICTIM ASSISTANCE

## Overview

Crime victim assistance in Egypt involves a mix of government services, civil society organizations, and international partners working to support those affected by violence, harassment, or trafficking. Victims can report crimes to the police by calling **122** or visiting a police station in person. In family courts across Egypt, Legal Aid Offices offer free legal services, including help with filing documents and court representation, especially in cases involving domestic violence or child custody. The **Ministry of Social Solidarity** (**MoSS**) operates shelters for victims of violence, including women and children, and opened its first shelter specifically for trafficking victims in Qalyoubia in 2020. These shelters offer psychological care, medical attention, and legal guidance.

Non-government organizations also play a crucial role. For example, the **Egyptian Center for Women's Rights** (**ECWR**) provides free legal consultations and awareness campaigns, and **HARASSmap** helps individuals report sexual harassment incidents and connect with support. The **Hisham Mubarak Law Center** offers legal aid in cases involving human rights violations, including torture or arbitrary detention. For migrants and refugees, organizations like the **International Organization for Migration** (**IOM**), **St. Andrew's Refugee Services** (**StARS**), and **Terre des Hommes** offer support including legal aid, mental health care, and shelter access. International efforts have supported Egypt's development of crime victim assistance. The **UN Women–USAID "Safe Cities"** initiative helped expand victim services, train police, and establish anti-harassment units in universities. It also helped the government criminalize harassment in 2014.

Despite these efforts, challenges persist. Many victims hesitate to report crimes due to fear of stigma or lack of confidence in law enforcement. Shelters, while available, vary in quality and accessibility. Compensation for trafficking victims, although authorized under Egypt's anti-trafficking law, is still pending implementation. Victims of sextortion or cyber harassment may seek help from informal online groups like Qawem, which assist in gathering evidence and pursuing legal cases. While the system continues to improve, navigating it may require persistence and the support of civil society networks.

## What to Do If You Are the Victim of a Crime

If you are the victim of a crime in Egypt, it's important to act quickly and follow specific steps to protect yourself, preserve evidence, and access the help available. First and foremost, **ensure your immediate safety**. If you are in danger, leave the area and go to a safe place. Call the emergency number **122** to reach the police. If you are a woman or child facing domestic or gender-based violence, you can also call **1366**, the Ministry of Social Solidarity's helpline for shelter and crisis support.

Make sure to **report the crime as soon as possible**. Go to the nearest police station or call 122 to file a complaint. Be prepared to give a statement and present any available evidence, such as medical reports, photos, or messages. In cases of physical or sexual assault, request a medical examination right away—preferably before bathing or changing clothes—to document injuries or collect forensic evidence.

If necessary, **seek medical help**. Hospitals in Egypt are legally required to treat victims of emergencies, including violence or assault. Ask for a copy of your medical report, as this may be important for your legal case. Also, **ask for legal aid** if needed. If you cannot afford a lawyer, you may qualify for free legal assistance. Family courts often have Legal Aid Offices that can help with documentation, protective orders, or representation. You can also contact organizations like the **Egyptian Center for Women's Rights (ECWR)** or the **Hisham Mubarak Law Center** for free consultations or legal help.

Do not hesitate to **seek psychological or emotional support**. If you're experiencing trauma, reach out to NGOs or hospitals that offer counseling. Shelters operated by the Ministry of Social Solidarity provide not only safe housing but also mental health care and social services. Finally, and very importantly, **preserve all documentation**. Keep copies of the police report, medical certificates, legal papers, and any messages or screenshots related to the crime. These may be critical if you pursue a case or need further protection. If you are a foreigner, **contact your embassy or consulate**. Most embassies can offer guidance, help you understand local procedures, and may connect you with translators or attorneys.

Taking these steps can help protect your rights and increase the likelihood of justice, even in a system that sometimes presents bureaucratic or cultural challenges. Let me know if you want a printable version of these steps or help locating services in a specific area.

## Common Tourist Scams in Egypt

Tourists in Egypt, especially in popular areas like Cairo, Luxor, Aswan, and the Red Sea resorts, may encounter a variety of scams that take advantage of inexperience or confusion. While many Egyptians are warm and welcoming, it's important to be alert to the common tricks used to exploit visitors. Here are a few of the most common tourist scams and how to avoid them.

One frequent scam involves **fake tour guides** or **overly persistent "helpers"** at tourist sites like the Pyramids of Giza or Karnak Temple. These individuals may claim to work for the site or government and offer to give you a tour, only to demand high fees afterward. Always book official guides through your hotel or a licensed travel agency, and ask to see their Ministry of Tourism ID.

Another common trick is the **"gift" scam**. A vendor, camel driver, or market seller may offer you a small item like a scarf, bracelet, or bottled drink as a "gift," only to later demand money for it. Politely refuse anything offered for free unless you're absolutely sure there are no strings attached. Equally widespread are **taxi scams**, especially at airports or near hotels. Some drivers refuse to use the meter and charge excessive fixed rates, or take longer routes on purpose. Use ride apps like Uber or Careem in Cairo and Alexandria, or insist on using the meter in white taxis. Always agree on the fare before entering if there's no meter.

In marketplaces (souks), some vendors quote **inflated prices**, especially when they sense a tourist is unfamiliar with the currency. Bargaining is expected, but if you're unsure, compare prices in a few shops first. Also beware of the "switcheroo" scam—where you agree on one item and are given a lower-quality substitute in the bag.

At cultural or religious sites, you might be approached by someone offering to "sneak" you into a closed area or let you touch something "sacred." This is usually followed by a bribe request or pressure to pay. Stick to the public areas and respect all signs or barriers. Another trick occurs at shops, especially perfume or papyrus stores, where tourists are brought in through a **"free tour"** or driver commission. You may be pressured into buying fake or overpriced goods. If you're taken to a shop unexpectedly, don't feel obliged to buy anything. Say no firmly and leave.

**Currency scams** can happen at exchange booths or when receiving change. Always count your money carefully and be familiar with the appearance of Egyptian bills—some scammers try to give you outdated or low-value notes. Also, be alert to "mistaken change" in taxis or shops where a large bill is handed over and the seller claims you gave a smaller amount.

In general, red flags include overly friendly strangers who approach you out of nowhere, people who insist you need their help, and situations where you're rushed or isolated. Trust your instincts, avoid giving out personal information, and when in doubt, walk away. To avoid scams, **do your research in advance, stick to reputable tour companies, carry small bills for transactions, and be polite but firm in saying no.**

Knowing the local customs and a few Arabic phrases (like *"la shukran"* – **"no, thank you"**) can also help you signal confidence and discourage scammers.

## Consular Assistance

If you are the victim of a crime while in Egypt, your embassy or consulate can offer critical support, though there are limits to what they can do. One of their primary roles is to help you understand and navigate the local legal system. Consular officers can explain your rights under Egyptian law, advise you on how to file a police report, and provide general information on what to expect during the investigation or any court proceedings. While they cannot intervene in legal cases, influence outcomes, or act as your lawyer, they can monitor your situation to ensure you are treated fairly and respectfully by local authorities.

If your passport is lost or stolen as a result of the crime, consular staff can help you obtain a replacement travel document so you can continue your trip or return home. They also assist with practical needs that might arise after a crime, including connecting you with local resources. Most embassies keep lists of English-speaking lawyers, translators, medical providers, and mental health professionals. If you've experienced a violent attack or sexual assault, they can refer you to clinics, counselors, or shelters, and may help arrange transportation to these services if needed.

In more serious situations—such as hospitalization, arrest, or trauma that leaves you unable to communicate—your embassy can notify your family or emergency contacts with your permission. They can't pay your hospital bills, legal fees, or buy you a plane ticket, but they can help you access funds from friends or relatives at home. In some cases, consular officers may accompany you to police stations or hospitals to make sure you're treated with dignity, especially if language barriers or cultural misunderstandings make things more difficult.

Overall, consular assistance is focused on safeguarding your well-being, helping you access local services, and making sure you aren't navigating a foreign legal and healthcare system alone. Their support can be a vital lifeline—especially when you're in a vulnerable position and far from home.

 **General Questions**

1. *If I am a victim of a crime, can I legally be compensated?*
In Egypt, victims of crime do not typically receive compensation directly from the state. Instead, under Egyptian civil law, **individuals can pursue financial compensation from the offender through civil court proceedings**, covering both material damages and moral harm. There are exceptions for certain crimes— such as human trafficking—where legislation provides for a dedicated victim compensation fund, though it may not yet be fully operational. Victims of torture and cruel treatment also have the right to seek compensation through legal claims. Because the process can be complex, seeking legal counsel is indeed advisable to navigate these claims effectively.

2. *If a family member falls victim to homicide, can I bring the body back to my home country?* **Yes.** If a family member is a homicide victim in Egypt, you can arrange to repatriate the body to your home country. This requires obtaining a death certificate, a transport permit, and completing any necessary investigations or autopsies. Your embassy or consulate can assist with paperwork and liaising with local authorities. You'll also need a licensed funeral service to prepare the body for international transport. The process can take time and may involve significant costs, so staying in close contact with your consulate is important.

3. ***What protections are in place to ensure the safety and confidentiality of crime victims during legal proceedings?*** In Egypt, protections for crime victims during legal proceedings include separate waiting areas and hearing rooms to reduce contact with the accused, especially in sensitive cases. Victims' personal information and medical reports are generally kept confidential. Female victims can be accompanied by a female relative or legal representative when testifying. While these measures exist, their application can be inconsistent, so NGOs and legal aid groups often help protect victims' rights and privacy throughout the process.

# POLICE

# CHAPTER 15

# POLICE

## Overview

Egypt's police force is **highly centralized** and operates under the authority of **the Ministry of Interior**, rather than being divided into separate federal, state, or municipal forces as seen in some other countries. Policing is structured regionally across Egypt's 27 governorates and their districts, but all these regional units report directly to the national Ministry. This centralization means that policies, training, and resource allocation are controlled at the national level, aiming for uniformity in law enforcement across the country.

The size of Egypt's police force is substantial, with estimates of around 450,000 personnel.[15] This includes a wide range of units such as the regular uniformed police, the Criminal Investigation Department (CID), traffic police, border security, and specialized riot control forces. Despite the large number of officers, questions remain about whether staffing levels are sufficient and appropriately distributed, particularly in rural or underserved areas where police presence can be sparse.

The force faces **several challenges**, including limited resources, outdated equipment, and inconsistent training standards. These factors can affect the ability of officers to respond effectively to crime and maintain public safety. In recent years, the government has launched initiatives

---

15   https://en.wikipedia.org/wiki/Egyptian_National_Police

to modernize the police force, improve training programs, and increase technological capabilities. However, debates continue among experts and citizens about whether these reforms have adequately addressed issues related to staffing shortages and operational effectiveness, especially given Egypt's large and growing population.

## Police Response

The Egyptian police serve as the country's primary internal security force and carry out a wide range of critical functions. These include maintaining public order, preventing and investigating crimes, regulating traffic, securing borders, enforcing judicial rulings, and protecting public institutions. They are also heavily involved in counterterrorism and national security operations, which often take precedence over community policing duties. In addition to uniformed police officers, the force includes investigative branches like the **Criminal Investigation Department** (**CID**), the **General Security Directorate**, and the **National Security Agency** (**NSA**), formerly known as the State Security Investigations Service.

One of the police's key roles is crowd control and riot suppression, particularly during demonstrations, elections, or periods of political tension. The **Central Security Forces** (**CSF**), a paramilitary branch with tens of thousands of personnel, often leads these operations. Police also operate in close coordination with the intelligence services when addressing organized crime, extremism, or perceived threats to the state. At the local level, police stations are responsible for day-to-day law enforcement, issuing ID documents, and responding to civilian complaints.

However, the Egyptian police face a number of deep-rooted challenges that impact both their effectiveness and public trust. A major issue is the **prioritization of regime security over community safety**. Since the 2011 revolution, the police have been increasingly tasked with maintaining political stability, which often leads to a heavy-handed approach, particularly in dealing with protests or dissent. This has fueled public mistrust and accusations of abuse, especially by units like the NSA, which have been linked to arbitrary arrests, surveillance, and torture.

Another significant challenge is the **lack of consistent training**, particularly in human rights, community engagement, and modern investigative techniques. Many officers are trained primarily in force and control, with limited exposure to forensic science or trauma-informed policing practices. Corruption and low wages also affect morale and accountability, with occasional reports of bribery or neglect of duty.

Additionally complicating the situation are **resource limitations**. While urban areas are relatively well-policed, rural and marginalized regions often experience inadequate coverage, slow response times, and poor infrastructure. This uneven distribution can lead to unequal access to justice, especially for women, minorities, or vulnerable communities.

Institutionally, the **absence of independent oversight mechanisms** weakens accountability. Complaints against police misconduct are often handled internally or dismissed altogether. Although Egypt has ratified several international human rights treaties, domestic enforcement of these standards remains inconsistent, and civilian access to legal recourse is limited.

## Police and Community Relations

The overall image of the police in Egypt is **complex and often divided**, shaped by decades of political history, personal experiences, and regional differences. Many Egyptians view the police with suspicion or fear, especially in urban centers and among political activists, journalists, and marginalized communities. This perception is rooted in a long-standing reputation for heavy-handed tactics, lack of accountability, and a focus on protecting the state rather than serving the public.

Public distrust of the police sharply increased after the 2011 revolution, which was partly fueled by anger over widespread police brutality, corruption, and arbitrary arrests under the Mubarak regime. The brutal killing of Khaled Said in 2010 by police officers became a national symbol of abuse and helped ignite the uprising (see Law of the Land True Story below). Since then, although some reforms have been introduced, including efforts to modernize the force and improve public engagement, many citizens still report fear of mistreatment, especially when reporting crimes or interacting with officers in lower-income areas.

In rural parts of Egypt, perceptions can be somewhat different. In some areas, local police officers are seen as more accessible or embedded within the community. However, their presence is often limited, and people may rely more on traditional dispute resolution or tribal mechanisms than on formal policing.

Women, LGBTQ+ individuals, and refugees often face specific challenges when dealing with police, including skepticism, dismissal of complaints, or even harassment. In cases of gender-based violence, some victims report being shamed, ignored, or discouraged from pursuing justice. Nevertheless, despite these challenges, there are parts of the population—especially those who prioritize security and stability—that hold a more favorable view of the police. For example, many Egyptians credit the police with helping restore order after the chaotic post-revolution years and view their tough approach as necessary in the fight against terrorism or street crime.

Internationally, Egypt's police are **widely criticized for human rights abuses**, including torture, arbitrary detention, and the suppression of political dissent. Organizations like Amnesty International and Human Rights Watch have documented systemic misconduct, particularly by the National Security Agency (NSA), which has been linked to enforced disappearances and mistreatment of detainees, including activists and minors. These concerns have contributed to Egypt's low rankings in global human rights and rule-of-law indexes.

Despite Egypt's strategic partnerships with countries like the U.S. and members of the EU—often based on counterterrorism and regional stability—foreign governments and international bodies have repeatedly called for reforms. Some aid and training programs continue, but they face criticism for potentially supporting repressive practices. Overall, the international view remains skeptical, urging greater accountability, transparency, and protection of civil liberties within Egypt's law enforcement system.

## Police Use of Force

Police use of force remains a **serious issue** in Egypt, with frequent reports of excessive violence, torture, and custodial deaths. Human rights groups, including Amnesty International and the Egyptian Initiative for Personal Rights, have documented **widespread abuse**, especially within police stations and detention centers. Methods include beatings, electric shocks, and prolonged suspension, often leading to injury or death.

Recent incidents also include the mass arrest and forced deportation of around 800 Sudanese refugees between January and March 2024. Amnesty International reported that police and security forces detained people in overcrowded and unsanitary conditions before deporting them without legal review, raising serious concerns about due process and the use of force. Excessive police action during protests continues to draw criticism, with officers using live ammunition, tear gas, and rubber pellets, leading to injuries and deaths. Accountability remains rare: of 135 officers tried for protest-related killings in recent years, most were acquitted.

While Egypt has announced reforms and modernization efforts, international watchdogs argue that these have not addressed the core issues—lack of transparency, institutional impunity, and the prioritization of regime security over civilian rights. Without independent oversight and stronger adherence to international standards, concerns over police violence are likely to persist.

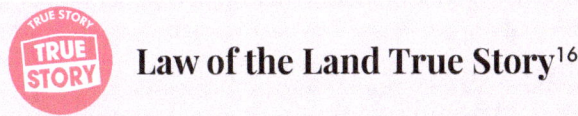

## Law of the Land True Story[16]

Khaled Mohamed Saeed, a 28-year-old from Alexandria, was beaten to death by plainclothes police officers on June 6, 2010, after allegedly refusing to show his ID outside an internet café. The police initially

---

16   https://www.cbsnews.com/news/
      the-deadly-beating-that-sparked-egypt-revolution/)

claimed he died from choking on drugs, but over twenty witnesses and circulating photos of his crushed skull, broken jaw, and facial fractures told a starkly different story.

These shocking images and eyewitness accounts ignited public outrage. Within days, a Facebook page called "We Are All Khaled Saeed," created by Google executive Wael Ghonim and activist Abdel Rahman Mansour, went viral. It quickly amassed hundreds of thousands of followers and became a hub for organizing protests and raising awareness about state violence. Silent vigils were held in multiple cities, and Khaled's name became a rallying cry for dignity, justice, and resistance against police brutality.

Khaled's death and the online mobilization it spurred helped galvanize the widespread protests on January 25, 2011, which ultimately forced President Hosni Mubarak's resignation. His case remains one of the most potent symbols of the abuses under the ancient régime and highlights the power of social media in modern political movements.

# HOW TO GET LEGAL HELP IN EGYPT

# HOW TO GET LEGAL HELP IN EGYPT

## Available Resources

If a tourist is arrested in Egypt, it is crucial to seek legal assistance immediately, as the country's legal system can be complex, especially for foreigners. The first step should be to **contact your embassy or consulate** since they can explain the basics of the local legal system, offer guidance on what to expect during police questioning or court appearances, and provide a list of vetted local attorneys familiar with representing foreign nationals.

Foreign visitors should also ask the police to allow them to **contact a lawyer directly**. Egypt does not have a formal duty lawyer system like some Western countries, but individuals have the right to legal counsel. It's important to find an attorney with experience in criminal defense and who is fluent in English or your native language.

 The U.S. Embassy in Cairo, for example, maintains a list of English-speaking lawyers on its website and can be accessed at **https://eg.usembassy.gov/wp-content/uploads/sites/197/2024/12/List-of-Attorneys-2024-Cairo-updated-1.pdf**.

Other embassies also maintain similar lists and can offer emergency support to citizens in distress.

When choosing a lawyer in Egypt, make sure to verify their license and experience, and be clear about fees, especially if a translator or additional services are needed. Many private lawyers in Egypt operate on a retainer or per-hearing basis. If cost is a concern, the consulate's list may include firms offering services at reduced rates for foreigners in difficult situations.

In emergency situations, international assistance organizations can also help. For example, **Fair Trials International**[17] offers guidance for individuals facing legal trouble abroad and may be able to assist with legal referrals or advocacy. The **International Committee of the Red Cross (ICRC)**[18] can intervene in situations of detention or alleged mistreatment and ensure the detainee's rights are being respected. In some cases, human rights NGOs in Cairo—like the **Egyptian Initiative for Personal Rights (EIPR)**[19]—may provide legal support or connect detainees to public interest lawyers, though availability is often limited due to political sensitivities and caseload.

Legal aid services in Egypt are **generally limited**, especially for non-citizens (see more information below). However, some universities and bar associations operate **legal clinics**, and a few NGOs offer limited assistance for cases involving human rights violations, trafficking, or asylum claims. Foreigners should not rely on free legal representation being available, so consular support and private legal counsel remain the most reliable options.

---

17   https://www.fairtrials.org/

18   https://www.icrc.org/en/contact

19   https://eipr.org/en

## Legal Aid

Legal aid in Egypt is extremely limited, especially for foreign visitors. While there is no explicit rule barring non-citizens from receiving legal assistance, in practice, **foreign nationals are rarely eligible for formal legal aid** through the state. Egypt does not have a nationwide legal aid system comparable to those in many Western countries. Most legal aid services are informal, inconsistently applied, and **generally reserved for Egyptian citizens** facing serious charges and unable to afford a lawyer.

For foreign visitors, access to legal aid is only possible in exceptional cases—typically when **serious criminal charges, detention, or alleged human rights** violations are involved. Even then, eligibility depends largely on the specific facts of the case, the individual's financial situation, and the willingness of independent organizations to get involved. There is no formal application process or clearly defined set of criteria. Instead, any assistance must usually be obtained through referral by a foreign embassy or a connection to a non-governmental organization that provides legal support.

If a foreigner does qualify for legal aid in Egypt, the support offered may include legal advice, representation during court hearings, and sometimes the services of an interpreter or translator. This assistance, however, is almost always provided by human rights organizations, university law clinics, or volunteer lawyers rather than a public defender's office. **These services do not extend to routine civil matters or commercial disputes, and they do not cover expenses like bail, court fees, or travel.**

## Foreign Embassies in Egypt

Foreign embassies and consulates in Egypt play a vital role in assisting their nationals who encounter **legal, medical, or personal emergencies** while abroad. While they do not have the authority to intervene in local legal proceedings or provide legal representation, but they can offer crucial support such as contacting family members, monitoring the treatment of detained citizens, ensuring access to legal counsel, and providing lists of local attorneys. They can also help replace lost or stolen passports, facilitate emergency travel documents, and issue guidance on local laws and customs. In the event of an arrest or detention, one of the most important services they offer is to make sure the individual understands their rights under Egyptian law and help ensure they are treated in accordance with international standards.

Egypt hosts over **140 foreign diplomatic missions**, including embassies, consulates, and permanent delegations. Most embassies are based in Cairo, primarily in the diplomatic districts of **Garden City, Zamalek, and Dokki**, while some countries maintain consulates in other cities like **Alexandria, Aswan**, and **Suez**, especially where tourism or trade activity is significant.

Among the most prominent diplomatic missions in Egypt are those of the **United States**, the **United Kingdom, Germany, France, Russia, China, Saudi Arabia**, and the **United Arab Emirates**. These embassies are considered especially influential due to a combination of political, economic, strategic, and historical reasons.

The United States maintains two main diplomatic posts in Egypt. The **U.S. Embassy in Cairo**, located in the Garden City neighborhood, is the primary mission and handles a wide range of services for American citizens, including consular support, legal referrals, and passport services. Its official website is **https://eg.usembassy.gov**. There is also a **U.S. Consulate General in Alexandria**, although its public services are limited compared to the embassy. Most routine and emergency services for American citizens are processed through the Cairo Embassy, including arrest or detention cases.

The U.S. Embassy in Cairo is one of the largest American diplomatic missions in the region, reflecting the deep military, security, and foreign aid ties between Egypt and the United States. It plays a significant role in regional diplomacy, counterterrorism cooperation, and development programs.

# MEDICAL FACILITIES & HOSPITALS

# MEDICAL FACILITIES & HOSPITALS

## Overview

Egypt's healthcare system is a mix of public and private services, with **varying standards** of quality and accessibility depending on location and economic status. While basic care is available to the general population, the overall system faces challenges such as underfunding, overcrowded public hospitals, and disparities between urban and rural healthcare access. In urban centers like Cairo and Alexandria, modern private hospitals offer high-quality services, often on par with international standards, especially for those who can afford out-of-pocket payments or have private insurance. In contrast, rural areas may lack adequate facilities, medical staff, and equipment.

The system operates through three main sectors: **public healthcare** run by the Ministry of Health, a network of **private providers**, and the new **Universal Health Insurance** (**UHI**) scheme, which is being rolled out gradually across the country. **Public hospitals** provide **subsidized or free care** but often suffer from long wait times and limited resources. The **private sector** is better staffed and equipped, offering a higher level of care, but at a **significantly higher cost**. Foreigners and tourists typically use private hospitals, and even many Egyptians opt for private care whenever possible.

Medical treatment in private clinics and hospitals is **generally affordable by Western standards**, with doctor visits costing between $10 and

$50 USD, and more specialized procedures priced significantly lower than in the U.S. or Europe. However, high-quality care in Egypt is only reliably accessible to those who can pay out of pocket or have private insurance.

In case of emergencies, the general medical emergency number in Egypt is **123**. For non-emergency medical inquiries, many private hospitals have their own hotlines. Ambulance response times can vary, and in critical cases, it may be faster to arrange private transport directly to a hospital, especially in busy urban areas. For police, the number is **122**, and for fire emergencies, **180**. These services generally operate in Arabic, so foreign visitors may need help from a local or hotel staff when calling.

## Visitors' Access to Healthcare in Egypt[20]

Visitors in Egypt can access medical services primarily through **private hospitals and clinics**, which are preferred by most tourists and expatriates due to their higher standards of care, shorter wait times, and greater likelihood of having English-speaking staff. These facilities are generally modern and well-equipped, especially in major urban centers like **Cairo, Alexandria**, and tourist hubs such as **Sharm El Sheikh, Luxor**, and **Hurghada**. While **out-of-pocket payment** is the most common method, many private hospitals also accept **international health or travel insurance**. However, it's important to note that direct billing is not always guaranteed—some facilities may require the visitor to pay upfront and then seek reimbursement from their insurer later. To avoid complications, travelers should check with both their insurance provider and the hospital about billing arrangements before seeking treatment, especially for non-emergency care.

Visitors are encouraged to carry documents related to their travel insurance, including policy numbers and emergency contact information. Some insurance policies require **preauthorization** for certain types of care, such as hospital admission or surgical procedures, so contacting the insurance company promptly is crucial. Many upscale hotels and

---

20  https://www.internationalinsurance.com/health/systems/egypt/

resorts also have arrangements with nearby private clinics and can help coordinate care for their guests.

In terms of **language barriers**, English is commonly spoken in private hospitals that cater to foreign patients. Medical staff, especially doctors and administrative personnel, are often fluent enough to handle consultations and paperwork in English. However, in **public hospitals and smaller local clinics**, English proficiency can be very limited, which may cause challenges in describing symptoms, understanding treatment plans, or following up on care. In such cases, visitors may need help from hotel staff, embassy personnel, or translation tools to communicate effectively.

The language gap can be especially problematic in emergencies, where time is critical. Some embassies advise their citizens to **carry a card that states any major medical conditions or allergies in Arabic, along with emergency contact information**. Using mobile translation apps or carrying a basic medical phrasebook in Arabic can also be helpful, particularly if traveling in rural areas or off the main tourist routes. For added peace of mind, travelers may consider visiting international medical centers that specialize in treating foreigners and offer services such as interpreter support, medical escorts, and multilingual documentation.

## Egyptian Hospitals

Egypt has a relatively large number of hospitals and medical staff overall, but there are significant disparities in distribution and quality. Most hospitals and specialized medical professionals are concentrated in urban areas, particularly in **Cairo**, **Alexandria**, and other major cities like **Giza** and **Helwan**. Rural and remote regions often face shortages of both hospitals and qualified healthcare workers, leading to limited access to advanced medical care outside the big cities.

**Public hospitals** form the backbone of Egypt's healthcare system and are widely available, but many are **overcrowded**, **under-resourced**, and suffer from **outdated equipment and infrastructure**. These facilities primarily serve the local population and generally offer free or low-cost care, though quality and wait times vary significantly. Some of the most reputable public hospitals include **Cairo University Hospitals, Kasr El Aini Hospital** in Cairo, which is one of the oldest and largest teaching hospitals in the region, and **Alexandria Main University Hospital**.

The **private hospital sector is more modern and better equipped**, offering higher standards of care, shorter wait times, and more comfort. Private hospitals tend to be clustered in affluent urban districts and tourist areas. Among the best private hospitals recognized for quality care and international standards are **As-Salam International Hospital, Cleopatra Hospital**, and **Al Mokawloon Al Arab Hospital** in Cairo, as well as **German Hospital Cairo** and **Dar Al Fouad Hospital**. These hospitals often have English-speaking staff, international patient services, and facilities that cater specifically to expatriates and foreign visitors. Many of these hospitals also accept international insurance and provide assistance with billing and insurance claims.

Egypt does not have an official American hospital in the sense of a U.S.-government-run medical facility, but there are several private hospitals with "American" in their names or branding that aim to offer services aligned with Western medical standards. For example, **American Hospital Cairo** is a private medical center that provides comprehensive healthcare services and markets itself to expatriates and foreigners. It is staffed with many internationally trained doctors and offers advanced medical technology.

## Insurance Guidance

Foreign insurance plans are **generally accepted by many private hospitals and clinics in Egypt**, especially in major cities and popular tourist areas. However, acceptance varies widely depending on the provider and the specific insurance policy. Some hospitals have direct billing arrangements with international insurance companies, allowing patients to receive treatment without upfront payment, while others require visitors to pay out-of-pocket first and then submit claims for reimbursement. It is important for visitors to confirm with both their insurer and the medical facility in advance to understand payment procedures and coverage details.

Medical costs in Egypt tend to be significantly lower than in Western countries. For example, a typical doctor's visit at a private clinic may range from approximately **$10 to $50 USD**, depending on the specialist and the clinic's reputation. Emergency room visits or more complex procedures, such as imaging or minor surgery, can cost several hundred dollars but usually remain affordable compared to prices in the U.S. or Europe. An emergency consultation might cost between **$50 and $200 USD**, while basic diagnostic tests or lab work can be **$20 to $100 USD**. Hospital stays and surgeries vary widely based on complexity, but private hospital prices generally remain lower than in Western healthcare systems.

Payment for medical services in Egypt is mostly done **upfront**, either by cash, credit card, or bank transfer. Many private hospitals accept major international credit cards, and some have partnerships with international insurers for direct billing, but these arrangements are not universal. Visitors should be prepared to pay at the time of service and keep all receipts and medical reports for insurance claims. It's advisable to carry sufficient funds or have access to credit to cover unexpected medical expenses. Some private hospitals also offer international patient services that can assist with insurance paperwork and billing.

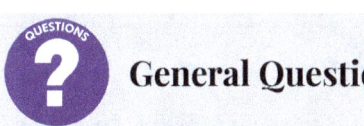 **General Questions**

1. *What number do I call in a medical emergency in Egypt?* In a medical emergency in Egypt, you should call **123** for an ambulance and emergency medical services.

2. *Will I be treated if I don't have insurance?* **Yes.** You will receive medical treatment in Egypt even if you don't have insurance. Public hospitals are required to provide emergency care

regardless of a patient's insurance or ability to pay. However, while emergency treatment is generally available, non-emergency services may require payment upfront. Private hospitals also treat uninsured patients but usually expect payment at the time of service.

3. *Can I find English-speaking doctors in Egypt?* **Yes.** You can find English-speaking doctors in Egypt, especially in private hospitals and clinics located in major cities. Many medical professionals in these facilities are trained abroad or have experience working with international patients, so they speak English well enough to communicate effectively. However, in public hospitals or rural areas, English proficiency among medical staff may be limited, so language barriers can sometimes be a challenge.

4. *Should I go to a public or private hospital?* Choosing between a public or private hospital in Egypt depends on your needs, budget, and the urgency of care. Public hospitals offer free or low-cost treatment and serve the majority of the population, but they are often overcrowded, have longer wait times, and may have outdated equipment and limited English-speaking staff. Private hospitals, on the other hand, provide higher-quality care, shorter waits, modern facilities, and better communication in English, making them the preferred choice for most foreign visitors and expatriates. If affordability is not a barrier and you want more comfort and reliable service, a private hospital is usually the better option. For emergencies or if cost is a concern, public hospitals can provide essential care but may require patience and assistance with language or navigation.

5. *Do I need to pay upfront for medical treatment?* **Yes.** In Egypt, you **generally need to pay upfront** for medical treatment, especially at private hospitals and clinics. Most facilities require payment at the time of service, either by cash, credit card, or bank transfer. Some private hospitals may have arrangements with international insurance companies for direct billing, but this is not common everywhere. Public hospitals typically provide emergency care regardless of payment ability, but non-emergency treatments may still require upfront payment. It's important

to be prepared to cover costs immediately or confirm payment terms with your healthcare provider beforehand.

6. *What if I need a prescription in Egypt?* If you need a prescription in Egypt, you can obtain one from a licensed doctor after a consultation at a clinic or hospital. Pharmacies are widely available and usually well-stocked with both local and imported medications. Many medications that require prescriptions in other countries may be easier to obtain in Egypt, but it's still advisable to get a proper prescription to ensure you receive the correct medicine and dosage. Pharmacists can often provide advice and may speak some English, especially in larger cities and tourist areas. For chronic conditions or specialized medications, bringing an adequate supply from home is recommended, as not all drugs may be available locally.

7. *Can I bring my medication to Egypt?* **Yes.** You can bring your personal medication to Egypt for your own use. It's important to carry medications in their original packaging, along with a copy of your prescription or a doctor's note explaining the medical need, especially for controlled or specialized drugs. Declaring your medication at customs can help avoid misunderstandings. If you require large quantities or injectable drugs, consult the Egyptian embassy or a healthcare professional beforehand to ensure compliance with local laws.

8. *What should I do in case of a medical emergency while traveling in Egypt?* In case of a medical emergency while traveling in Egypt, you should immediately call the emergency medical services number **123** to request an ambulance. If you're in a hotel or resort, alert the staff right away—they often have protocols for handling emergencies and can help arrange prompt medical assistance. If possible, contact your country's embassy or consulate to inform them of the situation; they can provide guidance, help coordinate with local medical providers, and offer support in case you need legal or logistical assistance.

# DRIVING IN EGYPT

CHAPTER 18

# DRIVING IN EGYPT

## Overview

Driving in Egypt is often described as a hectic and challenging experience, especially for foreigners not accustomed to local traffic habits. The overall driving environment is marked by **heavy congestion**, aggressive and sometimes **unpredictable driving behavior**, and **frequent disregard for traffic rules**. Drivers commonly use their horns, and lane discipline is loosely observed, which can be overwhelming for those used to more orderly road systems.

The road infrastructure varies significantly across the country. Major highways and roads connecting large cities such as Cairo, Alexandria, and the Suez Canal area are generally paved and maintained reasonably well. However, outside these urban centers, roads can be narrow, poorly marked, and in some cases damaged or filled with potholes. Rural and desert roads may have limited signage and lighting, making nighttime driving riskier.

Foreign drivers are required to carry a **valid driver's license** from their home country along with an **International Driving Permit** (**IDP**) recognized by Egypt. Additionally, vehicle registration documents and proof of insurance must be kept on hand at all times, as police frequently conduct document checks. **Insurance is mandatory**, and while basic coverage is often included with rental vehicles, visitors should confirm what is covered and consider additional insurance for peace of mind.

Egypt has **some unique driving customs**. For example, flashing head-lights is commonly used to signal "go ahead" or warn of obstacles. Drivers may also make informal hand signals or gestures that differ from international standards. Pedestrian crossings are often ignored, and jay-walking is frequent, so drivers must remain alert for sudden pedestrian movements. Traffic lights exist but may not always be strictly followed, so defensive driving is essential.

Regarding toll roads, Egypt operates **several toll highways,** including key routes like the Cairo-Alexandria Desert Road and the ring road around Cairo. Toll booths are typically staffed, and **payment is usually made in Egyptian pounds in cash.** Some toll plazas may accept electronic payment cards or prepaid passes, but cash remains the dominant method. It's advisable to carry small change to avoid delays. Toll fees vary depending on the road and vehicle type, but overall costs are relatively low compared to many other countries.

## Main Traffic Rules

- **Driving Side:** Right-hand side

- **Speed Limits:** Generally 50 km/h (31 mph) in cities, **90 km/h (56 mph)** on rural roads, and up to **120 km/h (75 mph)** on highways; however, enforcement can be inconsistent

- **Traffic Signals:** Standard traffic lights are used, but drivers often proceed cautiously even when signals are red due to common disregard; always be alert at intersections

- **Seat Belts: Mandatory for front-seat passengers;** enforcement varies, and rear-seat use is less commonly observed

- **Alcohol:** Strictly prohibited while driving; Egypt enforces **zero tolerance,** and penalties for driving under the influence are severe

- **Mobile Devices:** Use of handheld mobile phones while driving is illegal and can result in fines; hands-free devices are recommended

- **Toll Roads:** Several toll roads exist, with payment typically in cash at staffed toll booths; some accept electronic cards, but cash is preferred

- **If Stopped by Police:** Remain calm and polite, provide your driver's license, international driving permit, vehicle registration, and insurance documents when requested; avoid arguing and comply with instructions

- **Road Safety Tips:** Drive defensively and expect unpredictable behavior from other drivers and pedestrians; watch for sudden lane changes, use headlights when appropriate, and avoid driving at night outside urban areas due to poor lighting and road conditions

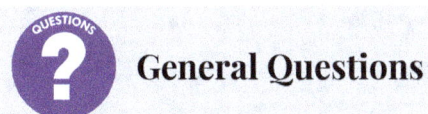 **General Questions**

1. *Can I use my driver's license from my home country to drive in Egypt?* **Yes.** You can drive in Egypt with your home country's driver's license, but you must also carry a valid International Driving Permit (IDP) obtained before arriving. The IDP acts as a translation and is required by Egyptian law. If your license isn't in English or Arabic, you'll need an official translation. Foreign visitors can use their license and IDP for up to six months; beyond that, you must get an Egyptian license, which involves tests and paperwork. Always carry your license, IDP, and any translations while driving in Egypt.

2. *What is the age requirement for renting a car in Egypt?* The minimum age to rent a car in Egypt usually ranges from **21 to 25 years,** depending on the rental company and vehicle type. Drivers under 25 may have to pay a young driver surcharge. Some companies also have a maximum age limit around 70 years and may charge fees for senior drivers. It's important to check the specific requirements with the rental agency before booking.

 **Law of the Land Hypothetical**

**HYPOTHETICAL**: *James, a British visitor, was driving in Cairo when he accidentally ran a red light at a busy intersection. A traffic police officer pulled him over and issued a fine on the spot. James is unsure whether he must pay the fine immediately or if there is an option to contest it. What are the legal procedures for handling traffic fines in Egypt, and what are the possible consequences if a driver refuses to pay a fine issued for a traffic violation?*

**ANSWER**: *In Egypt, when a traffic police officer issues a fine, the driver is generally expected to pay it promptly, often on the spot or within a short period. You can pay traffic fines through several convenient methods, primarily via the Public Prosecution website and the Egypt Digital Portal. Alternatively, Traffic fines can sometimes be settled at local police stations or authorized payment centers. Contesting a fine is possible but not commonly practiced, and the process can be bureaucratic and time-consuming.*

*If a driver refuses to pay a traffic fine, authorities may escalate the matter by increasing penalties or involving the traffic court system. Refusal to pay can lead to additional fines, legal complications, or even temporary detention, especially if the violation is serious or repeated. For foreign visitors, unpaid fines can cause issues with car rentals or future travel permissions, so it is advisable to settle fines promptly or seek legal advice if contesting the charge.*

# NUDE BEACHES & CLOTHING-OPTIONAL RESORTS

## IN THIS CHAPTER

- Overview
- Legality and Safety
- General Questions
- Law of the Land Hypothetical

# NUDE BEACHES & CLOTHING-OPTIONAL RESORTS

## Overview

Nudism is **not culturally acceptable** in Egypt. The country's deeply rooted conservative social norms, shaped by religious, cultural, and legal frameworks, strictly prohibit public nudity or any form of nudism. Egyptian laws explicitly forbid public exposure, and violations can result in legal penalties such as fines, detention, or imprisonment. Visitors and residents alike are expected to dress modestly in public spaces, including on beaches, at resorts, and in tourist areas.

Even at Egypt's most famous and internationally visited tourist destinations—such as the Red Sea resorts in Sharm El Sheikh, Hurghada, or Dahab—nudism remains strictly prohibited and culturally unacceptable. While these resorts tend to be more relaxed and welcoming to foreign visitors compared to other parts of the country, they still require modest swimwear at beaches, pools, and public areas. Many resorts enforce clear dress codes to respect local customs and avoid offending cultural sensitivities. Public nudity, including topless sunbathing, is not allowed. Although private villas or secluded spots may provide more privacy, visitors should exercise caution and avoid any form of nudity in visible or public areas to prevent potential legal issues or social backlash.

There are **no officially designated nudist beaches or resorts** in Egypt. All beaches, even those within private resorts, require proper swimwear, and topless sunbathing is generally frowned upon or outright prohibited. Hotels or resorts dedicated to nudism simply do not exist in Egypt due to the country's cultural and religious values.

## Legality and Safety

In Egypt, laws surrounding nudity and nudism are strict and clear: **public nudity is illegal and considered a violation of public decency and morality.** Egyptian legal codes prohibit any form of indecent exposure, which includes nudism, and such acts are punishable by law. Penalties can range from **fines and imprisonment to deportation for foreign nationals.** The severity of fines varies depending on the circumstances, while imprisonment can last for several months in more serious cases. Foreign visitors caught engaging in public nudity face not only legal penalties but also the risk of deportation and possible bans on re-entry.

These laws reflect the country's conservative cultural and religious values, which emphasize modesty and respect for social norms. There are no exceptions or designated areas where nudity or nudism is allowed, and enforcement is strict, especially in public and tourist areas. Beyond legal consequences, individuals may also face **social stigma and harassment.** Visitors are strongly advised to respect local dress codes and modesty standards to avoid serious legal trouble and personal risks.

Wearing revealing clothes in Egypt in general is frowned upon due to the country's conservative cultural and religious values, which emphasize modesty in public dress. While there is no legal prohibition against wearing revealing outfits, especially in major cities and tourist areas, doing so can attract unwanted attention, social disapproval, or even harassment. Visitors are advised to dress modestly—covering shoulders and knees—to show respect for local customs and avoid discomfort.

Likewise, modest swimwear is expected at beaches and pools throughout Egypt, including popular resort areas. Standard bikinis and one-piece swimsuits are widely accepted at private and hotel beaches, but topless sunbathing or nude bathing is illegal and socially unacceptable. At public beaches, more conservative swimwear is often preferred.

Visitors should always follow the dress codes set by individual resorts and be mindful of local sensitivities to avoid any issues.

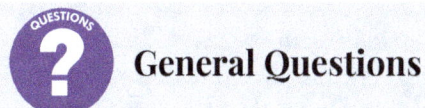 **General Questions**

1. *What are the best clothing choices for tourists in Egypt to respect local customs while staying comfortable in the hot climate?* The best clothing choices for tourists in Egypt balance respect for local customs with comfort in the hot climate. Lightweight, breathable fabrics like cotton or linen are ideal to keep cool while protecting the skin from the sun. Both men and women should aim for modest clothing that covers shoulders and knees, such as loose-fitting long pants, skirts, and tops with sleeves. For women, wearing a scarf or shawl can be useful for covering the head or shoulders when visiting religious sites. Light colors help reflect heat, and comfortable, sturdy footwear is recommended for walking. Dressing modestly not only shows respect for Egypt's conservative culture but also helps avoid unwanted attention, making the travel experience more pleasant and culturally sensitive.

2. *Are there any specific places in Egypt where tourists should be extra mindful about their clothing choices?* **Yes.** Tourists should be especially mindful of their clothing when visiting religious sites such as mosques, churches, and monasteries, as well as in rural or traditional communities. In these places, modesty is strictly observed, and visitors are expected to cover their shoulders, arms, and legs. Women may be required to wear a headscarf when entering mosques. Even outside religious sites, dressing conservatively in these areas shows respect for local customs and helps avoid offending residents.

 **Law of the Land Hypothetical**

**HYPOTHETICAL**: *Sarah, a tourist visiting Cairo, wears a sleeveless top and a short skirt while exploring the city's markets and historic sites. A local police officer approaches her and explains that her outfit is inappropriate and violates public decency. What are the legal standards regarding public dress in Egypt, and can tourists be penalized for wearing revealing or culturally inappropriate clothing in public?*

**ANSWER**: *In Egypt, the law does not specify exact dress codes, but public decency regulations are interpreted through the lens of conservative cultural and religious norms. Revealing clothing, especially in public or religious areas, can be considered offensive and a violation of public morality. While enforcement is typically mild—often limited to warnings or requests to dress more modestly—tourists can face consequences if their attire is seen as provocative or disrespectful. In more serious cases, particularly where behavior is also deemed disruptive, legal action such as fines or detainment is possible. To avoid trouble, tourists are advised to dress modestly, covering shoulders, cleavage, and knees in public areas, especially when visiting mosques, markets, and rural communities.*

# UNUSUAL LAWS

# UNUSUAL LAWS

## Overview

Unusual laws can be fascinating glimpses into a culture's values and history. While most people are aware of common legal restrictions, it's often the strange and quirky laws that capture our attention. These regulations can range from the amusing to the absurd, reflecting the unique circumstances and traditions of a place. Whether they arise from historical events, societal norms, or simply peculiar local customs, unusual laws can provide insight into the quirks of human behavior and governance.

 **Egypt's Unusual Laws & Associated Penalties**

Egypt has several laws that may seem unusual or strict to foreign visitors, many of which stem from the country's conservative values, religious principles, and emphasis on public order. While not all are commonly enforced, violating them can lead to serious consequences. Here are a few examples:

**Public Displays of Affection (PDA):**

Kissing, hugging, or other forms of public affection between couples—especially outside of marriage—are considered socially inappropriate and can attract police attention. While not always prosecuted, such behavior may result in **warnings, fines**, or, in some cases, **brief detention** for disturbing public decency.

**Taking Photos of Government Buildings or Security Personnel:**

It is illegal to photograph military sites, police stations, bridges, and government buildings. Taking photos of security officers or even police checkpoints without permission can lead to arrest, questioning, or having your equipment confiscated. Penalties may include **fines or short-term detention**, especially if authorities suspect the images could pose a security risk.

**Criticizing Religion or Promoting "Indecency":**

Speech or media seen as insulting Islam—or religion in general—can result in criminal charges under Egypt's blasphemy and morality laws. Similarly, promoting material considered "immoral" (such as LGBTQ+ content or adult-themed art) can result in prosecution. Penalties may include **fines, imprisonment**, or **deportation** for foreigners.

**Littering and Public Cleanliness Violations:**

Littering, spitting in public, or damaging public property can result in **fines** or **mandatory community service**. Although enforcement varies, authorities have increased efforts in recent years to penalize these behaviors, especially in tourist zones.

**Drug Laws (Including Medical Marijuana):**

Egypt enforces extremely strict anti-drug laws. Even small quantities of illegal substances, including cannabis or prescription medications without proper documentation, can lead to **arrest** and lengthy **prison**

**sentences**. Drug trafficking may carry life imprisonment or the death penalty.

**Same-Sex Relationships and "Morality" Charges:**

While same-sex relations are not explicitly outlawed, individuals suspected of being LGBTQ+ can be charged under "debauchery" or "immorality" laws. Arrests often stem from online activity or public behavior, with punishments including **imprisonment**, **fines**, or **deportation**.

These laws may seem unfamiliar to travelers from more liberal countries, but they are actively enforced in Egypt, especially if behavior is considered disruptive, indecent, or disrespectful to local norms. Visitors should remain aware of these regulations and always err on the side of caution to avoid legal issues.

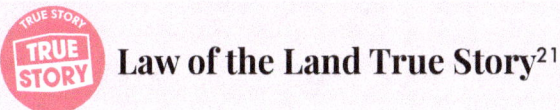 ## Law of the Land True Story[21]

In November 2018, 19-year-old British-Libyan student Muhammed Fathi AbulKasem was arrested shortly after arriving in Alexandria, Egypt. As his plane landed, he used his phone to record a video from the window, which happened to capture an Egyptian military helicopter. Egyptian authorities, enforcing strict national security laws that prohibit filming military equipment or personnel, interpreted the footage as a potential security threat. Upon landing, airport security detained Muhammed, seized his phone, and accused him of "collecting information against the military." His family learned about his detention only after hotel staff reported his failure to check in and expressed concern over his suspicious booking. Muhammed was held for nearly two weeks and brought before court multiple times. The

---

21   https://www.telegraph.co.uk/news/2018/12/10/
     british-teenager-released-two-weeks-hole-egyptian-prison

legal process was confusing and inconsistent—at one point, the lawyer initially assigned to his case abruptly withdrew, leaving him without clear representation.

Egypt's laws around national security and public decency are applied broadly, and even unintended violations—like filming near military infrastructure—can lead to serious consequences. Muhammed described his detention as extremely difficult and emotionally traumatic. After diplomatic pressure and public outcry, the charges were dropped, and he was released and allowed to return to the UK. He later thanked supporters for their advocacy but declined to discuss the conditions of his imprisonment.

The case served as a strong warning to tourists: **photographing or filming anything that could be seen as military or politically sensitive in Egypt can lead to arrest, prolonged detention, and prosecution under harsh national security laws.**

CHAPTER 21

# TRAVELING SAFELY

## IN THIS CHAPTER

- Ladies Traveling Solo
- Traveling as a Family
- Advice for All Travelers
- Do's and Don'ts While in Egypt

CHAPTER 21

# TRAVELING SAFELY

## Ladies Traveling Solo

Egypt has a rich and fascinating cultural heritage that draws millions of tourists every year, but its overall safety reputation is mixed. While many travelers have safe and memorable experiences, concerns about petty crime, harassment, and the unpredictability of local law enforcement often give Egypt a reputation for being less safe than other popular tourist destinations. It's not considered unsafe in the sense of widespread violent crime or civil unrest (except during rare periods of political tension), but travelers—especially women—are often advised to be extra cautious.

For women traveling alone, Egypt can present unique challenges. Harassment in public spaces is a widely reported issue, ranging from catcalling to more invasive behavior. While many local women dress conservatively and tend to avoid walking alone in some areas, solo female tourists may attract unwanted attention, particularly in crowded markets, public transportation, or tourist-heavy areas.

There are specific places that solo female travelers may wish to avoid or approach with caution. These include overly crowded areas like Cairo's downtown at night, rural or unlit neighborhoods, and poorly monitored side streets near bus or train stations. Beaches in certain coastal towns (such as parts of the Sinai Peninsula) have also seen occasional reports of harassment or theft. While many major tourist zones such as Luxor,

Aswan, and Giza are generally considered safe, even these can present occasional risks, especially after dark.

To stay safe, solo female travelers in Egypt should take several precautions. **Dressing modestly**—covering shoulders, cleavage, and knees—is one of the most effective ways to reduce attention and show cultural respect. It's wise to **avoid walking alone late at night, use reputable taxis or rideshare apps** (like Uber or Careem), and **stay in accommodations with good reviews and security**. Learning a few basic Arabic phrases and maintaining a confident, assertive demeanor can also help discourage unwanted interactions. Connecting with other travelers or joining guided tours for certain outings is another good strategy.

## Traveling as a Family

Egypt can be a family-friendly destination, especially for travelers interested in culture, history, and adventure. Children often find the ancient pyramids, camel rides, and boat trips on the Nile exciting and memorable. Resorts in areas like Sharm El Sheikh and Hurghada cater well to families with amenities such as kid-friendly pools, playgrounds, and entertainment programs. However, parents should plan ahead and be aware of health and safety considerations, as infrastructure and medical services may differ significantly from those in Western countries.

When traveling with children in Egypt, **food and water** safety is a major priority. Tap water should be avoided, and bottled or filtered water is the safest choice. It's also best to be cautious with food from street vendors—choose busy, clean-looking stalls and avoid raw produce unless you can wash or peel it yourself. The hot sun can be intense, so **children should wear sunscreen, hats**, and **lightweight protective clothing**, and drink water frequently to avoid dehydration.

Before travel, it's a good idea to visit a pediatrician to ensure your child's **vaccinations are current**. Bringing a basic medical kit with medications for fever, diarrhea, and allergies is helpful, as pharmacies may not always carry what you need. **Travel insurance that includes emergency pediatric care is highly recommended.** Egypt's traffic can be hectic and unpredictable, so always keep children close when walking near roads, and use car seats whenever possible. In taxis and local transport, car seats are rarely provided, but private transfers may offer them if requested in advance.

Sanitation can vary, so packing hand sanitizer, baby wipes, and tissues is essential, especially when using public restrooms. Egyptian people are generally warm and friendly toward children, but supervision is always important in busy places like markets or train stations. Teaching children to stay close and politely decline unwanted attention can also be helpful.

With the right preparation and precautions, Egypt can be an exciting and enriching destination for families traveling with children.

## Advice for All Travelers

Traveling in Egypt can be an incredible experience, but like in any foreign country, it's important to stay alert and be prepared for certain challenges. One of the main things to be cautious about is **scams**, especially in tourist-heavy areas like the pyramids, markets, and major landmarks. Some locals may approach you offering unsolicited help or tours, only to demand a tip or fee afterward. It's best to politely decline and only deal with licensed guides and official ticket counters.

Another major concern is **traffic**. Road conditions can be poor, traffic signals are often ignored, and drivers may not follow standard rules of the road. Pedestrians should be extremely careful when crossing streets and should never assume cars will stop. Use overpasses or cross with groups when possible.

**Petty theft**, including pickpocketing and bag-snatching, does happen, especially in crowded areas like bazaars, train stations, and public transportation. Travelers should keep valuables secure, avoid carrying large amounts of cash, and use anti-theft bags or money belts. It's also wise to make copies of your passport and keep the original in a secure place at your hotel.

Additionally, **cultural sensitivity** is another important factor. Egypt is a conservative country, and dressing modestly—especially outside of beach resorts—can help you avoid unwanted attention and show respect for local customs. Public displays of affection, drinking alcohol in non-designated areas, and disrespecting religious sites can all lead to trouble with authorities or locals.

Lastly, always **be cautious when discussing politics or religion**. Egypt monitors speech more closely than many travelers are used to, and critical comments—especially on social media—can lead to serious consequences. It's safer to avoid these topics altogether in public conversations.

By staying aware of your surroundings, showing cultural respect, and using common sense, most travelers to Egypt enjoy a safe and rewarding trip.

## Do's and Don'ts While in Egypt

To fully enjoy your trip and connect respectfully with locals, it's important to understand the country's social norms and expectations. From how you dress to how you interact with others, small gestures of cultural awareness can go a long way. Here are some key do's and don'ts to help you navigate Egyptian customs with confidence and respect.

### Do's

- Do respect prayer times and avoid loud behavior near mosques, especially on Fridays when many people gather for weekly prayers.

- Do dress appropriately when entering religious or traditional sites—men should also avoid sleeveless shirts and shorts in such spaces.

- Do keep a copy of your passport and visa with you, especially when traveling between cities or staying in hotels.

- Do use official transportation services when possible—apps like Uber or Careem are safer and more transparent than hailing taxis off the street.

- Do be friendly but cautious when engaging with strangers offering tours or shopping help, especially around tourist areas.

- Do keep hydrated and take breaks from the sun during midday, especially if traveling with children or older adults.

- Do tip service workers in hotels, restaurants, and for small acts of help—tipping is expected and appreciated.

### Don'ts

- Don't wear shoes inside mosques; always remove them at the entrance and dress conservatively to show respect.

- Don't assume people are okay with being photographed, particularly women—always ask first to avoid offending anyone.

- Don't engage in loud arguments or displays of anger in public— Egyptian culture values calm, respectful interactions.

- Don't ignore local customs—observe how locals behave and follow their lead, particularly in conservative towns.

- Don't carry large amounts of cash or flash valuables like expensive jewelry or electronics in public.

- Don't trust all "official guides" who approach you near tourist sites—some are not licensed and may overcharge.

- Don't expect everything to run on schedule—be patient and flexible; "Egypt time" can mean delays are common.

CHAPTER 22

# TOURIST TAXATION

IN THIS CHAPTER

- Overview
- Tourist Taxes in Egypt
- Law of the Land Hypothetical

# TOURIST TAXATION

## Overview

Tourism plays a vital role in Egypt's economy and is **one of the country's most important sources of income**. Before the COVID-19 pandemic, tourism contributed as much as 12% to Egypt's national GDP and employed millions either directly or indirectly through hospitality, transportation, and retail sectors. With its world-famous attractions like the Pyramids of Giza, the temples of Luxor, and the beaches of the Red Sea, Egypt continues to attract millions of visitors annually. The government has made tourism recovery and growth a top priority, seeing it as essential to long-term economic stability and job creation.

Generally, tourists are welcomed warmly by Egyptians. Locals in tourism-heavy areas often rely on visitors for their livelihoods and are eager to engage, offer services, or sell goods. While travelers may occasionally encounter aggressive sales tactics or scams, most Egyptians are hospitable, proud of their culture, and eager to share it with respectful visitors.

Tourist hotspots include Cairo, home to the Great Pyramids and the Egyptian Museum; Luxor and Aswan, rich with ancient temples and tombs; and Red Sea resorts like Hurghada and Sharm El Sheikh, popular for diving and beach vacations. These areas tend to be better equipped for tourists, offering a mix of modern amenities and historical attractions.

Tourists are **required to pay taxes** in Egypt—often included in hotel bills, airline tickets, and attraction entry fees—as a way to support the national infrastructure that accommodates millions of international guests. These taxes help fund the maintenance and development of public services, such as roads, airports, museums, and security, especially in tourism zones. They also contribute to environmental preservation efforts, particularly in places like the Red Sea, where coral reefs and marine life are major attractions.

In this way, tourist taxes not only sustain the quality of visitor experiences but also ensure that the benefits of tourism are reinvested into the country's future.

## Tourist Taxes in Egypt

Tourist taxation in Egypt is a routine part of travel and plays an important role in supporting the country's infrastructure, cultural conservation efforts, and public services that cater to millions of visitors each year. These taxes help maintain historic sites, improve transportation, and fund safety and sanitation in tourism-heavy areas. While these charges are **generally modest**, understanding them in advance can help travelers avoid surprises and better plan their budget.

 **Main Types of Tourist Taxes in Egypt**

- **Hotel and Accommodation Taxes:** Most hotels and guesthouses apply a combination of taxes to your stay. These typically include a service charge of around 12%, a municipality tax between 1–5%, and a Value-Added Tax (VAT) of 14%. Altogether, the total tax burden on a hotel bill can be around 26–31%, and while some hotels display prices inclusive of tax, others list the base rate and add taxes at checkout. Always review the booking details or ask for a full price breakdown in advance.

- **Value-Added Tax (VAT):** Egypt imposes a 14% VAT on most goods and services, including meals at restaurants, guided tours, transportation, and souvenirs. This tax is usually embedded in the listed price, though in more touristy areas it may appear as a separate line item. Foreign travelers are not currently eligible for VAT refunds when exiting Egypt, unlike in some other countries.

- **Departure Tax:** A departure tax may be levied when leaving Egypt, depending on your airline and route. Most commercial airline tickets already include this charge in the fare, but charter flight passengers or those flying from smaller regional airports should double-check their itinerary. The tax generally ranges from $20 to $25 USD but can vary.

- **Entry and Activity Fees:** Although not considered taxes in the strict sense, entrance fees at major tourist sites are a mandatory cost. These fees go toward site maintenance and tourism development. Examples include 540 EGP (about $11 USD) to enter the Pyramids of Giza complex or 600+ EGP (around $12 USD) to visit the Valley of the Kings. Some sites charge additional fees for photography or access to specific tombs or rooms. These prices are typically fixed and must be paid in Egyptian pounds.

- **Environmental and Marine Park Fees:** In Red Sea resorts like Sharm El Sheikh or Marsa Alam, tourists may be charged environmental protection fees when diving, snorkeling, or entering marine parks. These charges help preserve fragile ecosystems such as coral reefs and are usually collected by tour operators on behalf of the government.

These taxes and fees are almost always **applied automatically** and collected by businesses at the time of service. Tourists are not required to file any forms or pay taxes separately, aside from entry tickets or activities that are paid on-site. Being aware of these expenses allows visitors to understand not only the cost of their trip but also how their money contributes to the preservation of Egypt's landmarks, the improvement of tourism services, and the development of local communities that rely heavily on tourism income.

 **Law of the Land Hypothetical**

**HYPOTHETICAL**: *John, a tourist visiting Sharm El Sheikh, goes on a snorkeling trip arranged by a local tour operator. When paying, the operator adds an extra fee labeled as an "environmental protection tax." Is the environmental protection fee charged by the tour operator legal, and is John required to pay it even though it was not mentioned before booking?*

**ANSWER**: *Yes. The environmental protection fee is a legal charge in Egypt, especially in tourist areas like Sharm El Sheikh, where the government imposes such fees to help preserve coral reefs and marine life. Tour operators are authorized to collect this fee on behalf of the government. Even if the fee was not mentioned at the time of booking, John is required by law to pay it, as it supports environmental conservation efforts mandated by Egyptian authorities. However, tour operators should inform customers about such fees upfront to avoid confusion. John can politely request the operator to provide a receipt or official documentation for the fee. For future trips, it's advisable to ask about any additional charges before confirming a booking.*

# LONG-TERM STAYS

CHAPTER 23

# LONG-TERM STAYS

## Overview

Many people choose to stay long-term in Egypt for a combination of **financial, cultural, and lifestyle reasons**, but those who stay successfully often do so with a clear understanding of the practical realities involved. The country's **low cost of living** is one of its strongest attractions, especially for retirees, remote workers, and long-term travelers looking to stretch their budgets. In cities like Cairo or coastal towns like Dahab, daily expenses—from rent to food to transportation—can be a fraction of what they would be in Europe or North America. Healthcare is also affordable, and private hospitals and clinics in major cities like Cairo, Alexandria, and Sharm El-Sheikh offer good quality care, often with English-speaking doctors. Still, most foreigners prefer to carry international health insurance to ensure access to the best facilities. Pharmacies are widespread and many common medications are available without prescriptions, though it's wise to check availability of specific medicines in advance.

The decision to stay long-term is also often fueled by Egypt's **rich cultural and historical environment**. The country offers a sense of daily immersion in ancient civilizations, religious traditions, and a dynamic modern society. Expats and long-stay visitors often find meaning in studying Arabic, participating in community life, or simply exploring the rhythm of local customs. That said, adapting to the culture does take time. While Egyptians are known for their hospitality, the pace of life, gender norms, and religious observances may differ greatly from what some foreigners are used to. Understanding these dynamics—and approaching them with curiosity and respect—can significantly improve one's quality of life and relationships with locals. Women in particular may need to adjust expectations regarding dress and public behavior, especially in conservative areas.

Practical matters like visas and banking also play a role in long-term planning. Most visitors enter on a **tourist visa** that's **valid for 30 days** and can be extended, but those intending to stay longer should explore other options. While Egypt doesn't offer a formal retirement visa, some people obtain residency by working, studying, or owning property. Regulations can change, so it's wise to consult local legal help or embassy staff. Opening a local bank account generally requires a residency permit, but can simplify life by allowing you to pay bills and avoid international card fees. In the meantime, cash is still king in many places, though credit cards are becoming more common in big cities and tourist areas.

Safety and infrastructure are also important considerations. While major cities and tourist destinations are generally safe, foreigners are advised to avoid political protests and stay informed about current conditions. Petty theft like pickpocketing can occur in crowded areas, but violent crime is rare. Some remote regions, especially along borders or in northern Sinai, may carry travel warnings, so travelers should check with their embassy and local news before venturing far afield. Infrastructure in Egypt can sometimes be unpredictable—power outages, traffic congestion, and bureaucratic slowdowns are part of daily life. Those who thrive here tend to be flexible, patient, and resourceful.

Egypt has several **strong and active expat communities**, particularly in cities and regions that attract long-term foreigners due to work opportunities, tourism, or lifestyle benefits. While not as widespread as in some European or Southeast Asian countries, Egypt's expat communities are tight-knit, resourceful, and often very welcoming to newcomers. For example, **Cairo** hosts the largest and most diverse expat population in the country. This includes diplomats, aid workers, journalists, educators, businesspeople, and international students. There are well-established networks among Americans, Europeans, and Africans working in embassies, NGOs, universities, and multinational corporations. **Maadi**, a leafy suburb in southern Cairo, is one of the most popular neighborhoods for foreigners. It's home to international schools, expat clubs, yoga studios, and cafes that cater to Western tastes. **Zamalek**, an island in the Nile, is another favored area with art galleries, embassies, and upscale housing. These neighborhoods serve as social and cultural hubs where long-term residents gather for events, classes, and community support.

In **Alexandria**, the expat scene is smaller but still present, particularly among academics, language teachers, and those drawn to the city's literary and Mediterranean atmosphere. The American Center, British Council, and several universities host public lectures and English-language events that bring expats and locals together. The social scene here is more subdued than Cairo's but well-suited for those looking for a quieter, more intellectual expat experience.

**Dahab** has one of Egypt's most distinctive expat communities. This small town on the Sinai Peninsula is a magnet for divers, digital nomads, yoga teachers, and artists. Its relaxed pace, affordable cost of living, and natural beauty attract Europeans, South Americans, and others looking to live outside mainstream systems. The expat population here is highly international, and many have been in Dahab for years, running guesthouses, cafes, dive shops, or remote businesses. Community life revolves around beach gatherings, eco-projects, and informal coworking spaces.

**Sharm El-Sheikh** and **Hurghada** are popular with long-term residents from Russia, Ukraine, Italy, and Germany, many of whom came as tourists and stayed to work in the tourism sector or open small businesses. These resort towns are highly international, though the expat communities are often segmented by nationality and language group. Russian and Ukrainian enclaves are especially prominent, with local schools, media outlets, and shops catering to them. Also other towns like **Luxor** and **Aswan** also have small but tight-knit foreign communities, mostly made up of retirees, writers, and archaeologists. These communities often interact closely with locals and are drawn together by a shared passion for Egypt's ancient history and a slower, simpler way of life.

While Egypt's expat communities may not be as extensive or commercialized as in some countries, they offer genuine support, shared resources, and a welcoming atmosphere for those who plan to stay long-term. Online forums, Facebook groups, and in-person gatherings help newcomers connect, find housing, get visa advice, and build friendships. For many, these communities become an essential part of making life in Egypt not just livable, but deeply rewarding.

## Long-Term Visas

Egypt does not currently offer a dedicated long-term visa, however there are still viable pathways for foreigners who wish to stay in Egypt for an extended period—through renewable tourist visas, residency permits linked to employment, study, investment, or property ownership, and in some cases, by securing a work contract with a local organization.

Most visitors begin their stay with a **tourist visa**, which is either obtained on arrival (for eligible nationalities) or through an e-visa system online. This visa is usually **valid for 30 days**, but many long-term visitors simply extend it at Egypt's Mugamma office in Cairo (or its regional equivalents) or at local passport and immigration offices in other cities.[22] **Extensions** are generally granted for **three months** at a time and can be renewed repeatedly, though the process can involve long wait times, fees, and occasional bureaucratic hurdles.

For those seeking something more stable than repeated tourist visa renewals, Egypt offers a **residency permit**—known as an "**Egyptian Residence Permit**"—for foreigners who meet certain qualifications.[23] These include individuals working legally in Egypt, students enrolled in a recognized institution, spouses of Egyptian citizens, and property owners with proof of investment above a certain threshold. Residency permits are typically issued for one year and are renewable. Unlike tourist visas, these permits require more documentation, including a lease or property deed, health checks, police clearance, and sometimes bank

---

22  https://evisa-to-egypt.info/egypt-visa-extension/

23  https://evisa-to-egypt.info/blog/egypt-residency-and-work-authorization/

statements. Processing times can range from a few weeks to a couple of months depending on the region and visa type.

In addition, property owners—especially retirees—can apply for a **renewable residency permit**, though the requirements are not always consistently enforced. Generally, owning property valued at $50,000 USD or more can be grounds for applying, but policies vary. There is **no formal retirement visa category** in Egypt at this time, though some foreigners live in Egypt long-term through this informal route by continuing to extend their stays under residency tied to property ownership.

**Work visas** are another option, though these are typically sponsored by an Egyptian employer. The employer must apply through the Ministry of Manpower and Social Insurance, and the process includes labor market testing, background checks, and work permit issuance. Work visas are tied directly to the length of the employment contract and require a more structured legal and documentation process.

 To apply for tourist visas, the easiest route is through the Egyptian government's official e-visa portal at **https://www.visa2egypt.gov.eg.**

Applications can usually be processed within 3 to 7 business days. For residency permits or long-term stays, applications are submitted in person at the nearest **Passports, Immigration & Nationality Administration Office**. In Cairo, this is located in the Abbasiya neighborhood. Those applying in cities like Hurghada or Sharm El-Sheikh can use local branches, though wait times and service quality can vary significantly by location.

Processing fees depend on the visa type. A tourist visa extension typically costs around **1,650 EGP (roughly $35 USD**), while residency permits and work visas incur higher fees and may also require translation, medical, or legal processing costs. It's always recommended to bring multiple passport-sized photos, copies of key documents, and cash for payments.

Because rules and practices are not always uniformly applied, many long-term residents work with visa agents or immigration lawyers, especially if they are seeking residency on the basis of employment or property. Patience is key, but with the right paperwork and persistence, Egypt remains an accessible long-term living option for a wide variety of travelers and expats.

## Visa Application Requirements

To stay in Egypt legally—whether for tourism, study, work, or long-term residency—foreign nationals must meet a set of standard application requirements. The specifics vary depending on the visa type, but there are several documents and steps that are generally expected across most categories. All applicants must hold a **passport** that is valid for at least six months beyond the intended date of entry into Egypt. A **completed visa application form** is required, and this can be submitted either online (for e-visas) or in person at an Egyptian consulate or visa office. Most applicants must also provide at least one **recent passport-sized photo** (typically 4x6 cm, on a white background) and pay the **required visa fee**, which varies depending on the type and duration of the visa.

Tourist visa applicants generally need to show proof of accommodation (such as hotel bookings or a lease agreement), a return or onward travel ticket, and evidence of sufficient funds for the duration of their stay. While many nationalities are eligible for visas on arrival or through Egypt's official e-visa platform, others must apply in advance at an Egyptian embassy or consulate. A single-entry tourist e-visa costs **$25 USD**, while a multiple-entry visa is **$60 USD**.[24] These are typically valid for stays of up to 30 days and can be extended from within Egypt.

For long-term stays—such as study, work, or residency permits—**additional documentation** is required. This often includes a medical certificate, police clearance from your home country, proof of enrollment or employment, a rental contract or property deed, and bank statements showing sufficient financial means. Work visa applicants must also

---

24   https://visaindex.com/visa/egypt-visa/egypt-tourist-visa

provide a signed employment contract and have their employer apply for labor approval through Egypt's Ministry of Manpower. Students must submit an official acceptance letter from a recognized Egyptian educational institution.

Residency permit applications require proof of legal entry into Egypt (such as a valid visa stamp), along with a valid lease or proof of property ownership, copies of your passport and visa, and a utility bill in your name. Some applicants, especially those applying based on marriage or property investment, may also be asked to submit marriage certificates, title deeds, or bank records.

All visa and residency applications are submitted to the **Passports, Immigration & Nationality Administration Office** (often referred to simply as the "Mugamma" in Cairo) or its local equivalents. It's advisable to bring multiple copies of all documents, several passport-sized photos, and cash to cover processing fees. Translation of foreign-language documents into Arabic may be required in some cases, and it's generally safest to use a certified translator or legal office recognized by the Egyptian authorities.

While requirements are relatively straightforward, procedures can vary slightly depending on the location and the official handling your case. Because of this, many long-term residents recommend checking with the nearest Egyptian consulate before arriving or consulting with a local visa agent once in-country to help navigate the paperwork efficiently.

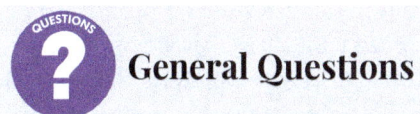 **General Questions**

1. *If I want to stay in Egypt for long-term and work, should I apply for a work permit before arriving in Egypt?* If you plan to stay in Egypt long-term and work, you technically need a work permit before starting employment, but most foreigners enter on a tourist visa and begin the process after arrival. Since the

permit must be sponsored by an Egyptian employer and requires in-country steps like medical checks and document translation, it's often more practical to handle everything locally. Your employer will submit the application, and you must wait for approval before working legally, though some people begin informally at their own risk. While you can start the process abroad, it's more common and flexible to complete it in Egypt once you have a job offer.

2. *I am American. Can I retire to Egypt?* **Yes.** As an American, you can retire to Egypt, but the country does not offer a specific retirement visa. Instead, retirees typically obtain renewable residency permits either by investing in property—such as purchasing real estate worth $100,000 USD or more—or by demonstrating a stable monthly income like a pension, usually around $1,000 to $1,500 USD. These permits allow for long-term stays and can be renewed annually or every few years depending on the investment amount. While residency does not automatically lead to citizenship, it does enable retirees to live in Egypt long-term with relatively straightforward paperwork.

## Law of the Land True Story[25]

In early 2024, Nigerian nationals residing in Egypt faced significant challenges due to a new government regulation requiring all foreigners to pay a $1,000 USD fee to renew their residence permits. The deadline for payment was set for March 13, 2024. However, authorities began enforcing this regulation before the deadline, leading to arrests and detentions of individuals who were unable to pay the fee. Many of those detained were reportedly subjected to harsh conditions in overcrowded cells. Instead of deporting detainees, the government

---

25  https://timeafricamagazine.com/nigerians-in-egypt-face-arrests-detention-over-inability-to-pay-1000-for-renewal-of-residence-permit)

reportedly kept them in prison until their families could raise the necessary funds for deportation and reimburse the expenses incurred during their detention.

This situation caused widespread panic among the Nigerian community in Egypt, as many individuals were unable to afford the fee, which was required to be paid in US dollars. The sudden implementation of this law, without prior notice, exacerbated the difficulties faced by Nigerians and other foreigners in the country. The Nigerian government expressed awareness of the issue but stated that it could not intervene, as the matter pertained to Egypt's domestic laws. The enforcement of this regulation highlighted the challenges faced by foreign nationals in Egypt, particularly amid the country's ongoing economic difficulties.

 ## Takeaways

- Many foreigners choose to stay long-term in Egypt because of the low cost of living, affordable healthcare, and rich cultural environment. Cities like Cairo and coastal towns such as Dahab offer daily expenses that are much lower than in Europe or North America, attracting retirees, remote workers, and long-term travelers.

- While Egypt does not have a dedicated retirement visa, long-term stays are possible through renewable tourist visas or residency permits linked to work, study, property ownership, or investment. The visa process can be bureaucratic and may require legal assistance, but with patience, long-term residency is achievable.

- Expat communities exist mainly in cities like Cairo, Alexandria, Dahab, and resort towns such as Sharm El-Sheikh and Hurghada. These communities provide social support and cultural connection, though their size and character vary widely depending on the location and nationality groups present.

- Practical challenges such as unpredictable infrastructure, occasional power outages, and bureaucratic slowdowns require foreigners to be flexible and patient. Safety is generally good in major cities and tourist areas, but remote or border regions may carry travel warnings.

- In early 2024, a new $1,000 USD fee imposed on foreigners for residence permit renewal caused significant distress among foreign nationals, particularly Nigerians. Enforcement led to arrests and detentions for those unable to pay, highlighting the financial and legal hurdles foreigners may face when trying to stay long-term in Egypt.

# CIVIL LITIGATION

# CIVIL LITIGATION

## Overview

Civil litigation provides a mechanism for resolving disputes, ensuring that travelers have a way to seek justice if legal issues arise while visiting another country. It helps them understand their rights and obligations under local laws, which may differ from those in their home country. The civil litigation system offers a formal process for addressing conflicts, such as contract disputes or personal injury claims, and can deter unfair practices by encouraging businesses to comply with legal standards. It also allows individuals to seek financial recourse for damages or losses and helps protect them from potential exploitation by local entities. Overall, understanding civil litigation enhances a visitor's experience and safety while traveling.

## Personal Injury Claims and Related Compensation

In Egypt, personal injury law is **governed by the Egyptian Civil Code**, not by a separate body of personal injury statutes like those found in some other countries. This means that injury claims are handled under general principles of civil liability—what's known as tort law. According to **Article 163** of the Egyptian Civil Code, any person who causes harm to another through fault or negligence is obligated to pay compensation. In order to bring a successful personal injury claim, the injured person must prove three things: that the other party committed a fault (which could include negligence, recklessness, or intentional wrongdoing), that real harm was suffered (such as physical injury, financial loss, or psychological trauma), and that there is a direct causal link between the act and the injury. Fault can be found in a wide range of incidents, such as car accidents, unsafe public property, falling construction materials, negligent security, or substandard medical care.

Tourists and foreign visitors in Egypt have the right to bring personal injury claims, but they should be aware of certain challenges. The Egyptian legal system is highly formal and court proceedings are usually conducted in Arabic, which means non-Arabic speakers will need legal representation and certified translations of documents. While Egyptian courts are open to foreign claimants, cases can move slowly and the procedures may be unfamiliar to visitors used to common-law systems. Most personal injury cases are heard in the civil courts, though if the injury stems from a criminal act—such as assault or reckless driving—the matter might be handled jointly in civil and criminal proceedings. Tourists should file a police report as soon as the injury occurs, collect any available medical records, and take photos or gather witness statements. These documents will be critical if the case goes to court.

Damages in Egypt are not calculated based on a fixed schedule. Instead, the judge determines the amount of compensation based on the evidence presented, which often includes expert testimony about the medical impact of the injury or the cost of care. Compensation can cover hospital bills, surgeries, lost income, long-term disability, disfigurement, and in some cases, emotional or psychological distress. In fatal accidents, the victim's family may also be eligible for moral damages, though courts often award relatively modest sums compared to U.S. standards. For example, in a2021 case, for example, awarded about $6,500 USD to a man injured by falling scaffolding due to a construction company's negligence—a meaningful amount in local terms but far lower than similar claims in other countries.

One important thing for travelers to understand is that **insurance coverage in Egypt can be inconsistent**. Many drivers, businesses, and even hotels may not carry liability insurance, and when they do, insurance companies often resist full payouts. Tourists should ideally carry **international travel insurance** that includes personal injury and liability coverage, especially if engaging in high-risk activities like desert safaris, scuba diving, or motorbike rentals. It's also important to understand that personal injury claims are subject to a three-year statute of limitations under Egyptian law, which means injured individuals generally have up to three years to file a claim from the date of the injury—or the date they became aware of the harm. However, evidence becomes harder to gather over time, so acting quickly is always best.

Finally, enforcement of court judgments can be another hurdle. Even if a plaintiff wins a case and is awarded compensation, collecting the money can be difficult if the defendant lacks funds or assets. Foreign plaintiffs especially may need local attorneys to monitor enforcement efforts or coordinate with Egyptian bailiffs. In cases involving hotels, tour operators, or businesses that cater to tourists, informal settlements are sometimes reached to avoid court altogether, especially when reputational damage is a concern.

## How to File a Civil Claim

Filing a civil claim in Egypt involves a formal legal process governed by the Egyptian Civil Procedure Code. Whether you're a local or a foreigner, the process is largely the same, though foreigners may face additional steps like document translation or hiring a licensed Egyptian attorney. Civil cases in Egypt are generally filed in either a **Primary Court** (**Mahkamat al-Bidaya**) or a **Court of First Instance**, depending on the **value of the claim** and the **type of dispute**. The court with jurisdiction is usually determined by the defendant's place of residence or where the dispute took place. For administrative cases (against government entities), the case may be filed at the **State Council** (**Maglis al-Dawla**).

Next, you must **prepare a formal statement of claim**. This document must clearly outline the facts of the case, identify the parties involved, state the legal grounds for the claim, and specify the remedy or compensation sought. The statement must be written **in Arabic**, signed by the claimant or their attorney, and supported by relevant documents such as contracts, receipts, police reports, medical records, or witness statements. Once the statement is prepared, it must be **filed with the court**

**clerk** along with **payment of court fees**, which vary depending on the nature and amount of the claim. In most cases, the fees are a percentage of the total amount being claimed. After filing, the court will issue a **case number and assign a hearing date**. The claimant must then ensure that the defendant is **formally served with legal notice** (known as a summons), typically through a bailiff or court officer.

During the **court proceedings**, both sides will have the opportunity to present evidence, call witnesses, and make legal arguments. **Civil trials in Egypt do not involve juries**; instead, the judge plays an active role in questioning the parties and evaluating the facts. Lawyers are not strictly required, but they are strongly recommended—especially for foreigners—because of the complexity of court procedures and the language barrier.

Once the trial concludes, the court will issue a **written judgment**, usually within a few weeks to a few months, depending on the court's workload. If the claimant wins, the court may order the defendant to pay compensation, return property, or take other corrective action. If either party disagrees with the ruling, they have the **right to appeal** to a higher court, typically within **30 to 60 days** depending on the type of case.

If the judgment is in your favor and becomes final, you may need to initiate **enforcement proceedings** to actually collect compensation or enforce the ruling. This is done through the **Enforcement Court**, which can seize assets, garnish wages, or take other steps to force compliance. Enforcement can be slow and challenging, especially if the defendant has limited assets or refuses to cooperate.

## Service of Documents

In Egypt, **service of documents**—meaning the official delivery of legal notices, court summons, or other case-related documents—is a **strictly formal and regulated process**, governed by the **Egyptian Civil Procedure Code**. It must be done properly for a case to proceed. If service is not completed according to the rules, a court may delay or even dismiss the case.

Service is handled by **official court bailiffs** or **process servers** employed by the court system. Private individuals or lawyers cannot serve documents themselves. Once a claim is filed, the court clerk issues a **summons** (called *judicial notification*), and forwards it to the bailiff department. The bailiff is then responsible for delivering the documents in person to the defendant. This is done at the **defendant's registered address**, which could be their home, workplace, or the address listed in the civil or commercial registry. The bailiff must physically go to the location and attempt to serve the documents directly to the person named in the case or someone authorized to accept on their behalf (such as a family member or office manager).

If personal service is not possible—say, the defendant is not present or refuses to accept the documents—the bailiff may **leave a copy at the address** and **post a notice on the door**. This is known as **constructive service**, and it is still considered legally valid. The bailiff then completes an **official service report** stating what happened during the delivery attempt, which is added to the case file as proof of service. If the defendant's address is unknown or outdated, the court may allow **service by publication**, which involves publishing the notice in two widely circulated Egyptian newspapers. However, this is considered a last resort and must be approved by the court. Service by email or postal mail is **not recognized as legally valid** in most civil cases in Egypt. For foreigners or entities located **outside Egypt**, service becomes more complex. In such cases, documents are often served through **diplomatic channels**—via the Egyptian Ministry of Foreign Affairs and the foreign country's embassy or consulate. Egypt is not a party to the Hague Service Convention, so international service must follow local diplomatic and bilateral agreements.

Once a document has been legally served in Egypt, **court proceedings can move forward—even if the defendant does not appear.** The court will consider the service valid as long as the proper procedures were followed and recorded. For anyone filing a civil case in Egypt—especially foreigners—it's essential to provide the court with a complete and accurate address for the opposing party and to follow up with court officials or a local attorney to ensure that service has been completed correctly and on time.

## Statute of Limitations

In Egypt, the statute of limitations—the legal time limit for filing a lawsuit—varies depending on the type of case, and is governed by the **Egyptian Civil Code**, specifically **Article 172**, and other applicable laws. In general, the standard limitation period for **most civil and commercial claims** is **15 years** unless otherwise specified.

For **personal injury claims**, including accidents and medical malpractice, the statute of limitations is **3 years** from the date the injured party becomes aware of the harm and the person responsible. **Contract disputes** usually fall under the 15-year rule, but commercial claims between traders may have a shorter limitation of **7 years**. **Labor disputes** typically must be filed within **1 year** from the end of employment, and **claims for unpaid wages** must be filed within **1 year** from when the payment was due.

In criminal matters, limitation periods differ by offense. For example, misdemeanors have a limitation of **3 years**, while felonies may carry a **10-year period**. However, the clock can be paused or reset in certain circumstances—such as if the defendant leaves the country or if legal proceedings begin before the time limit expires.

It's important to note that once the statute of limitations expires, the claim becomes inadmissible in court. Foreigners filing claims in Egypt should be especially mindful of these deadlines and consult a local attorney to ensure timely action.

 **Getting Married in Egypt**

Egypt is not widely known as a top international wedding destination in the same way as places like Italy, Greece, or the Maldives, but it does attract couples—especially from the Middle East, North Africa, and parts of Europe—who are drawn to its rich history, iconic backdrops like the Pyramids of Giza or the Nile, and luxury resorts in cities like Cairo, Luxor, Aswan, and Sharm El-Sheikh. While destination weddings in Egypt are less common for Western tourists, the country offers a unique setting for couples seeking something culturally distinctive or historically significant. Wedding tourism is growing, particularly for those looking for elaborate traditional ceremonies or luxurious desert and riverfront settings.

In Egypt, the process for getting married depends on whether the couple chooses a civil or religious ceremony. For foreigners, **only civil marriages** are legally recognized by the government. A civil ceremony must take place at the **Ministry of Justice in Cairo**, where both partners are required to appear in person and present documents such as valid passports, birth certificates, a certificate of no impediment from their embassy, and, if applicable, divorce or death certificates from prior marriages. All foreign documents must be translated into Arabic and notarized. **Religious ceremonies**, such as Muslim or Christian weddings, can still be held but do not have legal standing on their own for foreign nationals—they must be followed by civil registration to be valid in Egypt.

The official fee for registering a civil marriage is modest, typically between 200 to 500 Egyptian pounds (about $6 to $16 USD), but additional costs can arise from translation, notarization, embassy paperwork, and legal assistance, particularly for non-Egyptians. These extras can raise the total cost to anywhere between $100 to $300 USD or more, depending on the complexity of the case.

Once the civil marriage is performed, it is **registered with the Ministry of Justice** and the couple receives an official marriage certificate. If the couple intends to use the certificate abroad, it should also be **authenticated by the Egyptian Ministry of Foreign Affairs**. Most countries will recognize a properly registered Egyptian marriage, but it's important to check with your home country's embassy to confirm if further steps, such as local registration, are required. This is especially important for interfaith or dual-national couples, who may face additional bureaucratic requirements depending on where they plan to live or travel after marriage.

 **Law of the Land Hypothetical**

HYPOTHETICAL: *Carlos, a Spanish traveler, booked a Nile River cruise through an Egyptian tour company's website before arriving in Cairo. He paid in full online, but when he showed up on the scheduled date, the cruise was canceled without notice. The company refused to refund him, claiming the cancellation was due to "unforeseen weather conditions," even though local reports showed the cruise operated under clear skies on that day for other travelers. Can Carlos file a civil claim in Egypt to recover the money he paid for the canceled service?*

ANSWER: *Yes. Carlos has the right to bring a civil claim under Egypt's civil law, which allows individuals to seek compensation for financial loss caused by breach of contract or commercial fraud. If he can show that the company acted dishonestly or failed to deliver what was promised without valid justification, he may be entitled to a refund or additional compensation. To file the claim, Carlos would need to initiate proceedings in a local civil court, most likely in Cairo where the company is based. He must provide proof of payment, the original booking confirmation, any correspondence with the company, and a translated summary of local weather reports if relevant. Since the case involves a commercial dispute, court fees will be a percentage of the claimed amount. If successful, the court could order the company to return his payment and possibly cover additional damages. However, Carlos may face enforcement difficulties if the company lacks assets or tries to avoid payment, and it is strongly advised he work with an Egyptian attorney to navigate the formal process and ensure all documentation is properly submitted and served.*

CHAPTER 25

# OTHER THINGS TO KNOW

## IN THIS CHAPTER

- Tourists and Street Hustling
- Safety Concerns and Practical Tips
- In the Event of Death
- Experiencing Financial Hardship

# OTHER THINGS TO KNOW

## Tourists and Street Hustling

Street hustling is a widespread part of the tourist experience in Egypt, especially in popular destinations like Cairo, Luxor, Aswan, and the Red Sea resorts. Tourists walking near the Pyramids of Giza, the Egyptian Museum, or ancient temple sites often encounter persistent vendors, unofficial guides, camel ride operators, or shopkeepers who may follow them, strike up unsolicited conversations, or offer "free" services that later come with unexpected demands for payment. While some are friendly entrepreneurs trying to earn a living in a competitive market, others use high-pressure tactics, inflated prices, or misleading information to take advantage of visitors who are unfamiliar with local customs or the value of goods and services.

In legal terms, much of this activity exists in a gray zone. Egyptian law does not specifically ban street hustling, but it does prohibit fraud, harassment, unauthorized guiding, and misleading commercial behavior. Tourists who are victims of scams—such as being charged ten times the normal rate for a ride, sold fake antiquities, or deceived into handing over money under false pretenses—may have grounds for a complaint. These cases can be reported to the **Tourist Police**, a division of the national police force responsible for dealing with incidents involving foreigners. Officers are usually stationed around major attractions and in tourist-heavy neighborhoods. However, unless a crime is serious or well-documented, enforcement tends to be inconsistent, and tourists are often advised to seek informal resolutions or simply avoid confrontation.

To reduce the risk of being hustled, visitors should approach street in-teractions with caution. Politely declining offers, avoiding eye contact with aggressive vendors, and walking confidently can help. It's also es-sential to agree on prices in advance for things like taxi rides, camel or horse rentals, photo ops, or guided tours—even if someone claims it's free or included. Many travelers also benefit from using hotel-arranged transportation or guides, who are more likely to be licensed and ac-countable. Speaking a few basic Arabic phrases, such as "la shukran" (no, thank you), can deter some pushier hustlers. While street hustling is part of the travel experience in Egypt, being aware of local dynamics, know-ing your rights, and handling situations calmly can help tourists stay safe and avoid unnecessary stress.

## Safety Concerns and Practical Tips

Interactions with street hustlers in Egypt can sometimes go beyond an-noyance and pose real safety concerns. While most hustlers are nonvio-lent, tourists may feel overwhelmed or cornered by persistent vendors, fake guides, or scammers—especially in crowded or isolated areas. In rare cases, aggressive hustlers may grab a tourist's arm, block their path, or follow them for several blocks. There have also been reports of minor thefts, intimidation, or tourists being lured into overpriced services un-der false pretenses. Such encounters can leave travelers feeling vulnera-ble, especially if they're alone or don't speak Arabic.

To protect themselves, tourists should stay aware of their surroundings and avoid appearing uncertain or overly polite when approached. A firm but respectful **"no, thank you"** (*"la shukran"*) usually works best. Avoid accepting unsolicited help or following strangers who offer to guide you somewhere, even if they seem friendly. It's also smart to agree on prices before accepting any service, and to carry small bills to avoid disputes over change. Using licensed guides, taxis, or booking through hotels and reputable tour operators significantly reduces the risk of being targeted.

Tourists should also avoid displaying large amounts of cash, valuables, or expensive jewelry, which can make them more of a target.

Understanding local customs can also help tourists navigate interactions more smoothly. Egyptians are generally hospitable and enjoy conversation, so it's common for locals to strike up friendly chats. However, genuine hospitality is different from a hustle, and tourists should learn to distinguish between the two. In markets or busy tourist areas, bargaining is expected, but visitors should stay calm and walk away if they feel pressured. If a tourist feels harassed or scammed, they can report the incident to the **Tourist Police**, who are usually posted near major attractions, hotels, and transportation hubs. Tourists can also ask for help at their hotel reception or contact their embassy if they feel unsafe or need legal assistance.

 ## In the Event of Death

If someone dies while traveling in Egypt, the first step is to notify the local police so the death can be officially documented. You should also contact your country's embassy immediately. For Americans, that means calling the U.S. Embassy in Cairo at +20 (2) 2797-3300. The embassy can help notify next of kin, coordinate with local authorities, issue a Consular Report of Death Abroad, and provide guidance on local procedures. If the death occurs in a hospital, the staff will usually help facilitate this process and provide an initial death certificate in Arabic, which must be translated and notarized for use back home.

Egyptian authorities may require an autopsy, especially if the death was sudden or appears suspicious. The body cannot be repatriated or buried until the legal procedures are complete, and this can take several days. Transporting remains back to the U.S. or another country can cost between $5,000 and $15,000 USD, depending on the circumstances. Some travelers choose to arrange for local burial, but this involves additional steps and government permissions. Cremation is extremely rare in Egypt and often not permitted due to religious and cultural norms.

The embassy can also assist with the personal belongings of the deceased and help ensure they are returned to the family. They cannot get involved in Egyptian legal investigations but will monitor the process and stay in touch with the family. Travel insurance that includes repatriation coverage can significantly ease the burden. Before visiting Egypt, it is wise to register with the U.S. State Department's Smart Traveler Enrollment Program (STEP) and ensure that loved ones back home have copies of your passport and emergency contact details.

## Experiencing Financial Hardship

If you experience financial hardship while in Egypt, whether due to theft, unexpected expenses, or a lost wallet, it's important to act quickly and know your options. **Start by contacting your country's embassy or consulate.** For Americans, the U.S. Embassy in Cairo can assist in limited ways, such as helping you contact friends or family to send funds or providing information on how to receive money via services like Western Union or MoneyGram. While the embassy cannot give you money directly, they may help facilitate a wire transfer or coordinate an emergency loan in rare cases—typically to cover a plane ticket home if you agree to repay the government.

If you lose your credit or debit card, report it immediately to your bank to prevent fraud and request replacements. Many international banks and card providers can deliver new cards abroad within a few days. Money transfer services are widely available throughout Egypt, especially in major cities like Cairo, Luxor, and Alexandria, and often accept U.S. dollars or Egyptian pounds. If your hardship results from theft or a scam, file a police report as soon as possible; this may be necessary for insurance claims or embassy assistance.

Travel insurance, if purchased, may cover some emergency expenses related to lost funds, robbery, illness, or trip interruptions. Before traveling, it's wise to keep copies of important documents, a backup credit card, and emergency contacts separate from your main wallet. Understanding local costs and currency can also help you manage your budget while in Egypt. Being aware of exchange rates and typical costs helps you avoid overspending or falling victim to scams.

While Egyptian government agencies are unlikely to provide financial aid to foreigners, some **major tourist police stations**—especially in cities like Cairo, Luxor, Aswan, and Alexandria—may offer assistance in connecting travelers with their embassies or helping coordinate with hotels or local contacts in emergency cases. You can reach the Tourist Police by dialing **126** from within Egypt. **Hotels, hostels, and tour operators** are sometimes the most helpful first-line contacts. Many are accustomed to dealing with travelers in distress and may help you get in touch with your embassy, allow temporary stays while you resolve payment issues, or direct you to trustworthy services for currency exchange or money transfer.

Some large **religious organizations and churches**, such as Saint Joseph's Roman Catholic Church in Cairo or the Anglican Church in Zamalek, may occasionally provide short-term help or referrals to expat networks willing to assist. Similarly, Egypt has an active community of **expats and digital nomads** on platforms like Facebook and Couchsurfing, and reaching out to these groups may yield advice or local connections who can help.

If you find yourself in financial trouble, your embassy remains the safest first point of contact. They can connect you with available resources and support systems designed to assist travelers facing financial difficulties while abroad.

# QUICK REFERENCE GUIDE

- Quick Chapter References to Important Topics

# QUICK REFERENCE GUIDE

## Crime in Egypt

Are there particular areas I should avoid as a tourist?

> **Yes.** Tourists in Egypt should avoid the North Sinai region due to ongoing militant activity, and use caution in the Western Desert near the Libyan border, which has limited security. In cities like Cairo and Alexandria, it's best to steer clear of poorly lit or unregulated neighborhoods at night, such as parts of Ain Shams, Imbaba, or Moharam Bek. Stick to well-known tourist areas like Zamalek, Downtown Cairo, and Luxor, and avoid political demonstrations or remote travel without a licensed guide. *For more details, see Chapter 3.*

## Drug Offenses

Is the possession of marijuana legal?

> **No.** Marijuana is **illegal** in Egypt, and possession—even in small amounts—can lead to serious penalties, including up to three years in prison. While cannabis use exists discreetly among locals, especially in places like Dahab, enforcement can be strict and unpredictable, particularly for foreigners. Tourists should avoid all involvement with marijuana to prevent legal trouble.

Is the possession of cocaine legal?

**No.** Possession of cocaine in Egypt is **strictly illegal**, with penalties ranging from three years in prison for small personal amounts to life imprisonment or even the death penalty if it's deemed for trafficking. The law makes no distinction for tourists—any involvement with cocaine carries extremely severe consequences. *For more details, see Chapter 4.*

## Alcohol-Related Offenses

What is the legal drinking age?

The legal drinking age in Egypt is **21 years old**—this applies to purchasing, possessing, or consuming alcohol. You'll typically be asked to show ID in licensed hotels, bars, restaurants, and liquor stores in tourist areas. Drinking in public is prohibited, and stricter rules may be enforced during Ramadan, though exceptions exist for tourists in designated zones.

What is the legal blood alcohol limit to drive?

In Egypt, the legal blood alcohol concentration (BAC) limit for private drivers is **0.05%**, while **commercial drivers must maintain a 0.00% BAC**. Exceeding these limits can lead to fines, license suspension, and possibly imprisonment. Because enforcement can be strict and the driving environment unpredictable, it's safest to avoid drinking altogether if you plan to drive. *For more details, see Chapter 5.*

## Firearm & Ammunition Offenses

Can I possess a gun?

**No.** You **cannot legally possess** a gun in Egypt unless you are an Egyptian citizen with a special government-issued license, which is very difficult to obtain. Foreigners, including tourists, are not allowed to own or carry firearms under normal circumstances. Possession without a license is a serious offense and can lead to imprisonment, fines, or worse.

Can I possess ammunition?

No. You **generally cannot legally possess ammunition** in Egypt unless you hold a very special firearms license—something almost exclusively granted to Egyptian citizens for specific purposes. Foreigners, including tourists, are not permitted to own or carry ammunition. Doing so without proper authorization is a serious crime and can result in severe penalties. *For more details, see Chapter 6.*

## Prostitution

Is prostitution legal?

No. Prostitution is **illegal** in Egypt. Law No. 10/1961 criminalizes various activities related to prostitution, including operating or managing a brothel, soliciting, and living off the earnings of a prostitute. Penalties for these offenses can include imprisonment and fines. The law also criminalizes public solicitation and advertising of sexual services. While the act of selling sex itself is not explicitly mentioned in the law, these related activities effectively make prostitution illegal in practice. Enforcement of these laws can be inconsistent, and individuals involved in prostitution-related activities may face legal consequences. *For more details, see Chapter 7.*

## LGBTQ

Is homosexuality legal?

Homosexuality is **not explicitly illegal** in Egypt, but authorities often use laws against "debauchery" and "immorality" to arrest and punish LGBTQ individuals. Public displays of same-sex affection are strongly discouraged and can lead to harassment or imprisonment. There are no legal protections for LGBTQ people, and social stigma is high, so LGBTQ travelers should exercise extreme caution.

Are same-sex public displays of affection socially acceptable?

No. Same-sex public displays of affection are **not socially acceptable** in Egypt. They can attract negative attention, harassment, or even legal trouble due to strict social norms and laws targeting

LGBTQ behavior. It's best to avoid any public affection to stay safe. *For more details, see Chapter 8.*

## Arrested in Egypt

Would I be entitled to bail if I'm arrested?

**Yes.** As a foreigner arrested in Egypt, you may be entitled to bail, but this depends on several factors, including the nature of the alleged offense, whether you're considered a flight risk, and the discretion of the judge. While bail is legally permissible, it's not always granted, especially in cases involving serious crimes or national security concerns. However, there have been reports of individuals being detained beyond the legal limits, sometimes due to the addition of new charges.

Will a lawyer be provided to me if I cannot afford one?

**Yes.** As a foreigner arrested in Egypt, you are entitled to legal representation. Egyptian law mandates that every person accused of a criminal offense must have access to a lawyer. If you cannot afford one, the court is required to appoint a lawyer to represent you without charge. However, this provision may not always be enforced, especially in cases involving irregular immigration status or national security concerns. In such situations, it's advisable to contact your country's embassy or consulate, as they can assist in securing legal representation and ensuring your rights are upheld. *For more details, see Chapter 10.*

## Helping a Friend or Relative Imprisoned in Egypt

Can I send money to a friend or relative imprisoned in Egypt?

**Yes.** You can send money to a friend or family member imprisoned in Egypt, usually through bank transfers or money transfer services. However, it's important to follow the prison's rules and procedures, and it's a good idea to stay in contact with the prison or legal representatives to ensure the money is received properly.

Can I remain in the country upon release from prison or jail after my sentence is complete?

**Yes.** Once your prison sentence in Egypt is complete, you can generally remain in the country legally as long as your visa or residency permits are valid. However, if your visa has expired or you have outstanding legal issues, you may face restrictions or be required to leave. It's important to check your immigration status and ensure all paperwork is in order before your release. *For more details, see Chapter 12.*

## Crime Victim Assistance

Can a victim of a crime be legally compensated?

**Yes.** Victims of crime in Egypt can seek legal compensation through the courts. They may file a civil lawsuit against the offender to claim damages for physical, emotional, or financial harm suffered. However, the process can be complex and may require legal assistance to navigate effectively.

Does the Egyptian government offer assistance for family members of homicide victims?

**Yes.** The Egyptian government offers assistance to families of homicide victims, especially those killed in terrorism or military incidents. This includes financial compensation, medical care, scholarships, and housing support through a special fund. Additionally, compensation can sometimes be received through "diya" (blood money) paid by the offender's family. Families are advised to seek legal help to navigate these options. *For more details, see Chapter 14.*

## U.S. Consulate Assistance

Are there any limitations to the consulate assistance I can receive while in Egypt?

**Yes.** Consulate assistance in Egypt has limitations. While consulates can help with emergencies, provide legal referrals, and assist with communication, they cannot get you out of jail, provide legal representation, or intervene in local judicial decisions. Their support is limited by Egyptian laws and sovereignty, so it's important to understand they can offer guidance but not override local authority.. *For more details, see Chapter 14.*

## Police

Is there an official police force?

**Yes.** Egypt has an official police force called the **Egyptian National Police**, which is responsible for maintaining public order, enforcing laws, and providing security across the country. They handle everything from traffic control to criminal investigations. In case of a police emergency, dial **112** or **122**. *For more details, see Chapter 15.*

## How to Get Legal Help in Egypt

Is there a resource in Egypt to find legal representation?

**Yes.** There are resources in Egypt to help you find legal representation. You can contact your country's embassy or consulate for recommendations, and there are also local law firms and legal aid organizations that assist foreigners. Some NGOs and refugee support groups offer legal help as well, depending on your situation.

Is there free legal representation assistance?

**Yes.** Free legal representation is available in Egypt, especially for refugees, women, and those who cannot afford a lawyer. Various NGOs and organizations provide legal aid, but eligibility and services may vary.

Does my home country's embassy provide a list of local attorneys who speak English?

**Yes.** Your home country's embassy in Egypt can provide a list of local attorneys who speak English. For example, the U.S. Department of State maintains a list of foreign attorneys who have expressed a willingness to serve U.S. citizen clients. Similarly, the British Embassy in Cairo offers a list of English-speaking lawyers for British nationals.

These lists are available on the respective embassy websites and can assist you in finding legal representation in Egypt. *For more details, see Chapter 16.*

## Foreign Embassies in Egypt

Where can I find a complete and updated list of all diplomatic missions in Egypt?

List of diplomatic mission in Egypt is accessible at **http://www.eeca.gov.eg/empassy6.html**.

Where is the U.S. Embassy in Egypt located?

The U.S. Embassy in Egypt is located at 5 Tawfik Diab Street, Garden City, Cairo. The Consular Section can be reached at +(20) 2-2797-3300. For emergencies after hours, you can contact the same number. The embassy provides services such as visa applications, American Citizen Services, and emergency assistance. It's advisable to schedule an appointment in advance through their official website. *For more details, see Chapter 16.*

## Medical Facilities & Hospitals

Is there a number I can call for ambulance and fire emergencies?

**Yes.** In Egypt, you can call **112** for all emergency services, including police, fire, and ambulance. This unified number is part of Egypt's National Emergency Network, which aims to provide a streamlined response to emergencies. It is accessible 24/7 and automatically detects your location.

If I am injured while on vacation in Egypt, are there hospitals that are recommended for tourists?

**Yes.** Egypt has several hospitals recommended for tourists, especially in major cities like Cairo, Alexandria, and popular resorts. Many international and private hospitals offer quality care with English-speaking staff. It's best to use well-known facilities or those recommended by your embassy or travel insurance provider. *For more details, see Chapter 17.*

## Driving in Egypt

Which side of the road do I drive on?

In Egypt, you drive on the **right-hand side** of the road.

Can I use my driver's license from my home country to drive in Egypt?

**Yes.** You can use your valid foreign driver's license in Egypt for a short visit, but it's recommended to also carry an **International Driving Permit** (**IDP**) to avoid issues with local authorities. For longer stays, you may need to obtain an Egyptian driver's license.

How old do I need to be to rent a car?

The minimum age to rent a car in Egypt is typically **21**, though some rental companies may allow drivers as young as **18** to rent certain vehicle categories by paying a **"young driver fee,"** which can be up to 30% of the rental cost. Drivers under 25 are often subject to additional charges. *For more details, see Chapter 18.*

## Nude Beaches & Clothing-Optional Resorts

Is public nudity legal on the beaches?

**No.** Public nudity, including topless or nude sunbathing, is **strictly prohibited** in Egypt and is **considered illegal**. This applies universally, regardless of location, including private resorts or beaches. Engaging in such activities can lead to legal consequences, including fines, imprisonment, or deportation. It's essential to respect local customs and laws to ensure a safe and enjoyable visit. *For more details, see Chapter 19.*

## Tourist Taxation

Is there a room tax in Egypt?

**Yes.** Egypt has a room tax that applies to hotel stays. The tax rate is typically around 14% of the room rate and is included in the final bill at most hotels. This tax helps support local tourism infrastructure and services.

Is there any fee associated with leaving Egypt by air?

**Yes.** There is a departure fee when leaving Egypt by air. It's usually around 100 EGP (about $5.50 USD) and is typically included in your airline ticket price, so you don't usually pay it separately at the airport. Some tourists arriving through certain regions pay a reduced fee of about 50 EGP (about $2.75 USD). *For more details, see Chapter 22.*

## Long-Term Stays

Do I need to return to my home country to apply for a work permit in Egypt?

**No.** You **do not** need to return to your home country to apply for a work permit in Egypt. You can initiate the application process from abroad, but certain steps, such as undergoing a medical examination (including an HIV test) and obtaining a security clearance, must be completed within Egypt. Additionally, the work permit application is typically submitted by your employer to the Ministry of Manpower and Immigration in Egypt. While you can apply for the necessary entry visa from your home country, the final work permit process requires your presence in Egypt.

As an American, how long can I stay in Egypt without a visa?

As a U.S. citizen, you can stay in Egypt for **up to 30 days** without a visa by obtaining a visa on arrival at Egyptian airports or applying for an e-Visa online. Both options are valid for a single entry and cost approximately $25 USD. If you wish to stay longer, you can apply for a visa extension within Egypt, which may grant an additional

30 days, subject to approval by Egyptian authorities. *For more details, see Chapter 23.*

## In the Event of Death

What documents would an embassy need regarding the death of a tourist?

The embassy would need the official death certificate, the deceased's passport, a police or medical report, an embalming certificate if the body is being returned home, and contact details for the next of kin. *For more details, see Chapter 25.*

# EMERGENCY/IMPORTANT CONTACT NUMBERS IN EGYPT

 Please consider putting some of these numbers in your phone **prior** to traveling to Egypt.

## Emergency Numbers:

- **Police:** 122
- **Ambulance:** 123
- **Fire Service:** 180

## Other Useful Contacts:

- **General Emergency Services (combined emergency):** 112
- **Tourist Police (for traveler-specific issues):** 126
- **Coast Guard/Sea-rescue:** 114
- **Roadside Assistance (highway rescue):** +20 12 2111 0000
- **Ministry of Health Hotline:** 105 (for general public health advice, disease reporting, or COVID-related questions)
- **Poison Control Center (Cairo):** +20 2 2364 0825
- **Egyptian Red Crescent (Egypt's version of the Red Cross):** +20 2 2598 5555

## Legal Assistance:

- **Egyptian Bar Association:** https://egyls.com
- **Digital Legal Aid Platform (Microjustice Egypt):** +20 110 211 8923, email info@microjusticeegypt.org

# USEFUL EGYPTIAN ARABIC ('AMMIYA) PHRASES

## Greetings

HI/HELLO – Ahlan / Salaam – أهلاً/ سلام

GOOD MORNING – Ṣabāḥ el-kheir – صباح الخير

GOOD AFTERNOON – Masā' el-kheir – مساء الخير

GOOD NIGHT – Tisbaḥ ʿalā kheir – تصبح على خير

GOODBYE – Maʿa el-salāma – مع السلامة

## Magic Words

PLEASE – Law samaḥt (to a man) / Law samaḥti (to a woman) – لو سمحت / لو سمحتي

THANK YOU – Shukran – شكراً

YOU'RE WELCOME – ʿAfwan – عفواً

CHEERS! – Fī saḥitak! – في صحتك!

EXCUSE ME – ʿAfwan / El-maʿzara – عفواً/ المعذرة

## Getting Around

WHERE IS THE BATHROOM? – Fein el-ḥammām? – فين الحمّام؟

WHAT TIME IS IT? – El-sāʿa kām? – الساعة كام؟

HOW DO I GET TO...? – Arooh ez-zāy...? – أروح إزاي...؟

WHERE DOES THIS TRAIN/BUS GO? – El-ʿarabeya dih rāyha fēn? – العربية دي رايحة فين؟

RESTAURANT – Maṭʿam – مطعم

HOW MUCH DOES THIS COST? – Bikām dah? – بكام ده؟

TRAIN/METRO STATION – Maḥaṭṭit el-ʿatr / el-metrō – محطة القطر / المترو

## Communication

DO YOU SPEAK ENGLISH? – Bititkallim Ingilīzi? (to a man) / Bititkallimi Ingilīzi? (to a woman) – بتتكلم إنجليزي؟ / بتتكلمي إنجليزي؟

I DO NOT UNDERSTAND – Ana mish fāhim (male) / Ana mish fāhima (female) – أنا مش فاهم / أنا مش فاهمة

I DON'T SPEAK ARABIC – Ana mā-bitkallimsh ʿArabī – أنا ما بتكلمش عربي

I DON'T KNOW – Maʿrafsh – معرفش

## Emergency

HELP! – El-ḥaʿūnī! – الحقوني!

CALL AN AMBULANCE! – Itṣil bi-ʾs-sayāra el-esʿāf! – اتصل بالإسعاف!

I NEED A DOCTOR – Ana meḥtag daktōr – أنا محتاج دكتور

POLICE – El-bolīs – البوليس

I'M LOST – Ana dayiʿ (male) / Ana dayiʿa (female) – أنا ضايع / أنا ضايعة

IT'S AN EMERGENCY – Dī ḥāla ṭawārī! – دي حالة طوارئ!

# GLOSSARY

**ACQUITTAL**: A jury verdict that a criminal defendant is not guilty, or the finding of a judge that the evidence cannot support a conviction.

**ADVERSARY PROCEEDING**: A lawsuit arising from a controversy that begins with filing a complaint.

**AFFIDAVIT**: A written statement made under oath.

**APPEAL**: A request made after a trial court has decided against one party in which the losing party asks a higher court to review the decision for legal error.

**ARRAIGNMENT**: A proceeding in which a criminal defendant is brought to court, told of the charges, and asked to plead guilty or not guilty.

**BAIL**: The temporary release of a person from jail when awaiting trial, on condition that a sum of money be lodged or deposited to guarantee an appearance in court.

**BARRISTER**: A lawyer admitted to plead at the Bar and who may try cases in superior court.

**BURDEN OF PROOF**: The duty to prove disputed facts.

**CAUSE OF ACTION**: A legal claim in a civil action.

**COMPLAINT**: A written statement that begins a civil lawsuit in which the plaintiff details the claims.

**CONTRACT:** An agreement between two or more persons to do something or to not do something.

**CONVICTION:** A judgment of guilt against a person charged with a crime.

**CUSTOMS DUTY:** A tariff or tax imposed on goods when transported across international borders.

**COURT LIAISON:** A person that coordinates with attorneys to perform administrative duties, such as scheduling witnesses, sharing information with law enforcement, and overseeing the reporting of cases to foreign embassies when applicable.

**DAMAGES:** Money that a defendant pays to a plaintiff in a civil case if the plaintiff wins.

**DEFENDANT:** 1) The individual against whom a civil claim is filed; 2) The individual against whom a criminal claim is filed.

**FELONY:** A serious crime, punishable by more than one year in prison.

**MAGISTRATE:** A judicial officer of a district court, who conducts initial proceedings in criminal cases, decides criminal misdemeanor cases, conducts many pretrial civil and criminal matters on behalf of district judges, and decides civil cases with the consent of the parties.

**MISDEMEANOR:** An offense punishable by one year or less in jail.

**PLAINTIFF:** A person or business that files a formal complaint with the court.

**PLEA:** In a criminal case, the answer of "guilty," "not guilty," or "no contest" in response to a criminal charge.

**SOLICITOR:** A lawyer who advises clients, represents them in lower court, and prepares cases for barristers to try in higher courts.

**SOVEREIGN IMMUNITY**: A legal doctrine by which the sovereign or the state (i.e. government) cannot commit a legal wrong and thus, it is immune from criminal and civil liability and cannot be sued.

**STATUTE**: A written law passed by a legislative body.

**STATUTE OF LIMITATIONS**: A statute prescribing a period of limitation to bring certain types of legal actions. If the action is not brought within that time, the person or entity (in a criminal context) is permanently barred from suing in court.

**SUBPOENA**: A command, issued under court authority, for a witness to appear and to give testimony.

**TESTIMONY**: Evidence presented orally by witnesses.

**VERDICT**: The decision of a judge or jury in a case.

**WARRANT**: Court authorization to conduct a search or to make an arrest.

# ACKNOWLEDGMENTS

This book series would never have seen the light of day without the able assistance of the following people:

**Kathy Adams**, my paralegal for over 22 years, who is the "Best" I've ever worked with during my entire legal career because of her amazing work ethic, organizational skills, and her ability to think outside of the box in unique and creative ways;

**Ally Knez-Siddique**, a professional writer, and one of my paralegals, whose eye for detail, according to her, is both a blessing and a curse;

**Gino Ibanez**, my former law clerk, whose exceptional research skills helped move this book series along in its early stages;

**Rosa Diaz Graham**, my legal assistant who helped with research and word processing at the very beginning of this project;

**Shelia Martin**, one of my former paralegals, worked diligently on this series of books, even after taking on another job. Her organizational skills are reflected throughout;

**Mindy Scarlett**, my marketing and publishing "Guru"! Her creativity and vision have no boundaries!

# ABOUT THE AUTHOR

**Michael L. Moore** practices in Orlando, Florida, the city where he spent his formative years. He credits the trauma of having his brother murdered when he was only 10 years old, as the catalyst that drew him into the practice of law.

Moore attended Florida State University, where he was a member of the FSU debate team. Upon graduating, he was awarded a full scholarship to attend the University of Tennessee College of Law, where he was elected President of the Student Bar Association. He further honed his advocacy and public speaking skills by participating in 'moot court' competitions.

After clerking at the Tennessee Attorney General's office while in law school, Moore moved back to Orlando, Florida, to work at the State Attorney's Office as a prosecutor, and where he was fortunate enough to meet the young lady that would eventually become his wife. Moore moved on to working for private law firms, both local and national, and eventually established his own law firm in 1999. He continues to make Orlando his home base.

It was the murder of a close friend and client in Jamaica that caused Moore to realize that books on laws in other countries were few and far between, and he was inspired to create Law of the Land Publishing. Moore launched Law of the Land Publishing to provide a series of guidebooks and a membership site for tourists and business travelers to stay up to date on the laws in each country they travel to, as well as having access to assistance if they run into legal issues.

"My vision is to educate people on what their legal rights are, and how they can access legal assistance, no matter where they have to travel to in the world," said Moore. "As Americans, we have a right to due process, but in some countries, you don't even have the right to access a square meal when incarcerated. My goal is to provide the information needed to stay out of trouble, as well as having access to assistance if trouble finds you."